Victory Over Death

BY KEITH MOORE

VICTORY OVER DEATH

© 2020 Keith Moore

ISBN: 978-1-940403-03-8

BK805

Faith Life International, Inc.
6009 Business Boulevard
Sarasota, FL 34240
941-702-7390
www.moorelife.org

Table of Contents

Chapter 1: To Die Is Gain

First Corinthians 15:57 says, "But thanks be to God, which giveth us the victory through our Lord Jesus Christ." That was, and still is, one of Brother Kenneth E. Hagin's favorite verses. He and I would be just walking down the hall, or walking to the car, or getting on the plane, and suddenly, he would just begin to say that. "Thanks be to God which giveth us the victory through our Lord Jesus Christ." I say it myself like that quite often.

He is the God Who gives us the victory, and it is through our Lord Jesus Christ. This is a familiar verse to many, and people have quoted it in connection to victory over sickness and pain, victory over financial lack, victory over depression and problems—and I believe that's all true. But in this chapter, he was talking about a specific thing over which the Lord has given us victory: death. We just read verse 57, so that means there are 56 verses leading up to this powerful summary statement.

I want to go back and begin reading with verse 1. He said, "Moreover, brethren, I declare unto you the gospel which I preached unto you, which also ye have received, and wherein ye stand; By which also ye are saved, if ye keep in memory what I preached unto you, unless ye have believed in vain. For I delivered unto you first of all that which I also received, how that Christ died for our sins according to the scriptures; And that he was buried, and that he rose again the third day according to the scriptures: And that he was seen of Cephas," that's Peter, "then of the twelve: After that, he was seen of above five hundred brethren at once; of whom the greater part remain unto this present, but some are fallen asleep. After that, he was seen of James; then of all the apostles. And last of all he was seen of me also, as of one born out of due time." He's saying Jesus died, but He was raised from the dead. He said that Peter saw Him, and the 12 disciples saw Him, and then 500 people saw Him at one time, then James saw Him, and then Paul saw Him himself. Paul said he saw Him after He had died, after He was raised from the dead. You recall that he saw Him on the road to Damascus, and he saw Him other times after that.

His Resurrection Is Our Victory

Look at 1 Corinthians 15:12. "Now if Christ be preached that he rose from the dead, how say some among you that there is no resurrection of the dead?" Apparently there were some people who were saying there was no resurrection. Paul went on to say, "But if there be no resurrection of the dead, then is Christ not risen: And if Christ be not risen, then is our preaching vain, and your faith is also vain."

Now friend, it doesn't get any more important than this. Was He or was He not raised from the dead? If He wasn't raised from the dead, you shouldn't be in church, and all preaching is a waste of time. Every denomination, every group, every church is a farce;

there is nothing to it. It doesn't get much more important than this. Did He raise from the dead?

You'll hear some people say, "Well, we're not all in agreement on these spectacular, supernatural things. A literal, physical resurrection from the dead?" I've heard people say, "We disagree on some of those things, but that's not the most important thing. The most important things are the teachings of Jesus. What He taught is important." No, you're wrong. If He didn't raise from the dead, there is no salvation. There is no church. No—this is all important. He said that if He didn't raise from the dead, our preaching is in vain. Your faith is in vain. This whole thing is for nothing if Jesus didn't raise from the dead. What do you think? Did He or didn't He?

Verses 14-20 continue, "And if Christ be not risen, then is our preaching vain, and your faith is also vain. Yea, and we are found false witnesses of God; because we have testified of God that he raised up Christ: Whom he raised not up, if so be that the dead rise not. For if the dead rise not, then is not Christ raised: And if Christ be not raised, your faith is vain; ye are yet in your sins. Then they also which are fallen asleep in Christ are perished." That's the end. "If in this life only we have hope in Christ, we are of all men most miserable. But now is Christ risen from the dead..." He did, He has, He is. It makes all the difference whether you believe that or not. It is not optional. If you want to live, if you want to be saved, if you want a future in eternity, you have to get this settled forever. He was born of a virgin. He *did* die and bear my sins and yours. He was raised from the dead, and He's alive and coming back again.

Christ is risen from the dead, and He's not the last One to be raised from the dead—He's just the first One. Verse 20 continues, saying, He is the "...firstfruits of them that slept." What does that mean? What happened to *Him* is going to happen to *you*, and to me. I like this already!

Continue reading verse 21. "For since by man came death, by man came also the resurrection of the dead. For as in Adam all die, even so in Christ shall all be made alive. But every man in his own order: Christ the firstfruits; afterward they that are Christ's at his coming. Then cometh the end, when he shall have delivered up the kingdom to God, even the Father; when he shall have put down all rule and all authority and power. For he must reign, till he has put all enemies under his feet. The last enemy that shall be destroyed is death." (vv. 21-26) Death is not a friend. Death is an enemy, and it is the last enemy that's going to be done away with, that will be put underfoot.

Death Is an Enemy

I have heard preachers say that a person was given peace by "sweet death." Death is an enemy. There's a reason why our natural body and everything about us naturally resists death and recoils from death. We weren't made to die. We were made to live forever.

It's only because of sin that death is in the world, and that death has passed upon all men—because all have sinned, the scripture says. (Romans 5:12)

But there is coming a time when death, the last enemy, is going to be destroyed. After that, there will be no more dying. Now that's kind of hard for us to understand because the whole time we've been on this planet, everything around us is dying. Everything is dying. The planet itself is groaning and creaking. Tornadoes, storms, and other problems with the weather are not the good pleasure and will of God. The planet is experiencing some of the same effects as our bodies. Our bodies are made out of the materials of the planet, and the Bible says the earth is groaning and travailing. Why? It's dying.

But God is going to fix everything. Soon and very soon, there will be no more death. That means plants don't die and animals don't die; nothing dies. The grass never dies. We've never been in a place like that, but we are going to be—where nothing ever dies. Death will be no more. It will be a thing of the long-forgotten past. No more dying. Death is an enemy—the last enemy that shall be destroyed.

Skip to verse 35. "But some man will say, How are the dead raised up? and with what body do they come?" This is unbelief and sarcasm. Some might question, *"We buried him fifty years ago. His body is decomposed. How is he going to be raised up?"* The response is in verse 36. "Thou fool, that which

thou sowest is not quickened, except it die: And that
which thou sowest, thou sowest not that body that
shall be, but bare grain, it may chance of wheat, or
of some other grain: But God giveth it a body as it
hath pleased him, and to every seed his own body."
He said it's like a seed: when you plant it, it dies,
but that's not the end of it; out of that death comes a
new plant and a new life.

Continue reading verse 42. "So also is the
resurrection of the dead. It is sown in corruption; it
is raised in incorruption: It is sown in dishonour; it
is raised in glory: it is sown in weakness; it is raised
in power: It is sown a natural body; it is raised a
spiritual body. There is a natural body, and there is
a spiritual body. And so it is written, The first man
Adam was made a living soul; the last Adam was
made a quickening spirit. Howbeit that was not first
which is spiritual, but that which is natural; and
afterward that which is spiritual." (vv. 42-46) So we
are experiencing the natural now. But our bodies are
going to be changed and are going to become
spiritual bodies, no longer subject to corruption and
decay. That includes aging—aging is decay. This is
just as true as Jesus being raised from the dead
because that's what this is based on. If you believe
He was raised from the dead, then you believe that
what happened to His body is in *your* future.

Philippians says that our bodies are going to be
changed and made just like His glorious body. The
Bible calls our current condition "vile." It is.
Anything that is dying is stinky. That is all we've

been exposed to in this life. I'm sure if we could leave all of this and stay out for a while, then come back, we would say, "No, don't make me go back to that stinking, vile, corrupt, decaying dying place." That's where we are for now.

But by the grace of God, we can run our race and finish our course. We can believe Him for healing and repair work and strength and whatever it takes to finish our race. But this is what we have to look forward to: incorruption and immortality.

We Will Be Changed

Verse 49 continues, "And as we have borne the image of the earthy, we shall also bear the image of the heavenly," just like Jesus' body. "Now this I say, brethren, that flesh and blood cannot inherit the kingdom of God; neither doth corruption inherit incorruption." We can't enter into the glory of God—into heaven or into the new city—in our current condition. It's too corrupt. It's been too affected. It has to be changed. He said, "Behold, I shew you a mystery; We shall not all sleep, but we shall all be changed, In a moment, in the twinkling of an eye, at the last trump: for the trumpet shall sound, and the dead shall be raised incorruptible, and we shall be changed." (vv. 49-52)

Say this out loud: **I'm going to be changed.**
How quickly will we be changed? Blink your eyes: changed. This is not a fairy tale. Soon and very soon, this is going to happen. The trumpet is going

to sound, the power of God is going to hit you, it's going to go over your body, and your body is going to be changed at a level we can't even measure. It will no longer be mortal. It will no longer be subject to pain, decay, or corruption. You will finally have a body that can keep up with your re-created human spirit. You will have a body just like Jesus' body. He did some amazing things after He was raised from the dead: He went to heaven, He came back, He went, He came back, He went through walls, and He appeared in different forms. He appeared one way this time, and He appeared another way another time. Just like changing your hairstyle. You can just look different because you feel different, I guess. He looked amazing and radiant. He also ate fish and honeycomb. We still get to eat!

This is our future. This is not a fairy tale. This is reality in God.

Death Is Swallowed Up

He went on to say in verse 53, "For this corruptible must put on incorruption, and this mortal must put on immortality. So when this corruptible shall have put on incorruption, and this mortal shall have put on immortality, then shall be brought to pass the saying that is written, Death is swallowed up in victory." *Swallow* means "gulp completely." That means victory is going to gulp up death, and it will be no more. Death will be forever destroyed and defeated, and there will be no more death. Nothing will ever die again. Do you believe it? We can believe all of this because our Lord was raised from the dead. That's why we can believe it: It has already happened. It's not *going to* happen. It *has* happened. It has already happened!

Death is swallowed up in victory. You can tell Paul has "preached himself happy." He gets sassy. He said, "O death, where is your sting? O grave, where is your victory?" Where is your bite? Grave, you don't have victory!

Skip to verse 57. "But thanks be to God, which giveth us the victory through our Lord Jesus Christ." In light of all this, what victory is he talking about? Victory over death. We have it through our Lord Jesus Christ because He obtained victory. He died, but then He rose triumphant over death. Thank You Lord!

Now, if we have victory over death, it should not be a terror to us. The Bible talks in Hebrews about the fear of death and how it makes a person subject to bondage their entire life. You are not free to live until you are no longer afraid to die. As long as you are afraid of death, it will warp your life. It will keep you in a form of dread. Some people are either dreading themselves dying or dreading someone around them dying, and they act like the worst thing that could possibly happen is to die. They talk about death as though it is "the end." Termination. Death is not termination. Death is transition. It's not "the end." It is simply a transition out of here to there. The Bible calls it a "departure."

Births are arrivals. Deaths are departures, not terminations. You are just leaving one place and going somewhere else. That's not a fairy tale or a theory. That's reality.

If that's true, and we do have victory over death, then why would we be tormented by it? Why would we be tortured by it? Why would we pace the floor and wring our hands and say, "Oh no! They may die!" Why would we say, "What if they tell me I'm going to die? I may die!" Let me clear it up for you: There is no "may" about it. If the Lord tarries His coming, you're going to die. Not maybe; you are. How many people are alive still that lived in the 1300s? Or in the 1400s or the 1500s? How many are alive today that lived in the 1700s? If the Lord tarries His coming a couple hundred years from now, how many of us will be here? In 200 years, how many of us will be here? Not a one.

Now we know the Lord could come, and if He comes and catches us away, that would be amazing. But if He tarries just a very short time, we are going to die. Are you believing to live a long, full life? The scripture says, "With long life He will satisfy you." (Psalm 91:16) That doesn't mean you will live forever, but a long, full life. That means you're going to a lot of funerals. If you live a long time, you're going to outlive a lot of your friends and family, maybe siblings and others. Is that going to torture you? Is the grief going to incapacitate you? We should not act shocked when someone dies.

Death: The Way of All the Earth

When David was about to die, he said this: "I go the way of all the Earth." (1 Kings 2:2) We are told, from a recent census, that there are over 7.7 billion people on the planet right now. People are dying every day. Out of seven billion people on the planet, how many are dying? It is a regular thing that people die on planet Earth. We're told that on average, every second, two people die somewhere in the world. By the time you finish reading this chapter, over 6000 people will have died. Before the day is over, about 156,000 people will have died. In a year, about 57 million. Over fifty million people will die in a year. Pretty soon, we will, too. Should that scare us? Should that trouble us?

There are many people, Christians included, who are just tortured by the thought of death and will do anything to try to add another few days down here, like that's all there is. No, life down here is the briefest thing we will ever do.

Psalm 90:1 begins, "Lord, thou hast been our dwelling place in all generations. Before the mountains were brought forth, or ever thou hadst formed the earth and the world, even from everlasting to everlasting, thou *art* God." (vv. 1-2) How long *has* He been around? Everlasting. How long *will* He be around? Everlasting. How long is that? We don't know. We can't put it on a clock or a calendar.

Verse 4 continues, "For a thousand years in thy sight *are but* as yesterday when it is past, and *as* a watch in the night." A thousand years, ten centuries, a millennium to God is like yesterday. That is His perception of the passing of it. And of course, He is right.

So if you live one hundred years, that is a tenth of a day in His perspective. That would be like living a couple of hours—and a lot of folks don't make it that long.

So yes, the Lord *is* coming back again, and there will be those who are alive and remain and will be caught up together with Him and be changed. But if He tarries, in His time—just a couple of minutes—that could be too long for us. We are greatly looking forward to His return on the one hand, but on the other, we want more time, because we want everybody to be saved who can be saved. The reason why He hasn't already come back is because of His long-suffering, the Bible says. He is not willing that any should perish. (2 Peter 3:9) He is letting this go on to give people more time to come to Him and get to know Him, and future generations.

Life Is Brief

But, the scripture says, "What is your life? It's a vapor, or a mist, that appears for a little while and then disappears." (James 4:14) It lasts just a couple of hours, from God's perspective.

If you say, "I don't like to talk about this…," that is what I'm talking about. You need to get free. When you get to thinking right, it won't bother you at all to talk about it.

Psalm 90:12 continues, "So teach us to number our days, that we may apply our hearts unto wisdom." *Number* means "to count." Are you keeping track of your days? Are you counting the days? There is a countdown to when you're out of here. Are you counting them off?

Sometimes people say, "I don't like to think about that." You need to think about this because the Bible says to count our days, to number them.

Verse 12 in the New Century Version says, "Teach us how short our lives really are so that we may be wise." This has to do with wisdom. If you don't keep yourself aware of how few days you have left, you will squander your time. You will waste it on things that mean nothing. It is precious time that you cannot get back.

Wake up every day realizing that you don't have many days left to do things down here, just a handful. And you need to do what you are supposed to do—what you were put here to do—because soon and very soon, you will be out of here. Your life is like a two-hour mist, and you may have already spent an hour of it. Some people have already spent an hour and fifty minutes…. But that doesn't have to scare you or trouble you.

I'm not scared. How about you? It does not depress me. Why? Because "thanks be to God, which giveth us the victory through our Lord Jesus Christ." (1 Corinthians 15:57) He died, but He isn't dead. He rose from the dead. He didn't do it for Himself. He didn't need it. He did it for you, for me, for us. His victory over death is our victory over death. And when you know the truth, you can stand by the graveside of someone dear to your heart, and even though you have feelings, and a tear may come down your cheek, you stand there and say, "Death! Where is your bite? Grave! Where is your victory? This is not the end." It is sown in corruption, but it is raised in incorruption. It is sown in weakness, but it is going to be raised in power and glory. The trumpet is going to sound, and the dead in Christ are going to rise. All of us are going to be changed, and death will be no more. (1 Corinthians 15:52)

The New Living Translation of Psalm 90:12 says, "Teach us to realize the brevity of life, so that we may grow in wisdom."

Our life on the earth is the briefest, shortest thing we will experience. I know it seems like a long time, but it's only because this is all we have ever experienced. Soon and very soon we're going to find out what all of this is about. Our minds and our hearts are going to be expanded like the oceans. I think for the first century or two in heaven, we're just going to be saying, "Wow! Oh wow!"

But friend, part of our witness in this life is that we are not afraid of death like others are. We don't mourn and grieve like those who have no hope— because there *is* hope. There is a future. The grave is not the end. (1 Thessalonians 4:13-14) We should not be shocked or surprised when someone dies. We should be aware of it and know that it is happening all around us. We should know that it's nothing new.

If your mom dies, or your dad, or your brother or sister or friend or whoever it is—you have a soul, and you're having some feelings, but you also have to remember that scores of thousands of people all over the planet experienced the same thing today. They experienced the same thing yesterday, and will experience the same thing tomorrow. We should have known they're not going to live down here forever. Neither are you, nor am I. We know it's coming, and soon, so we need to be numbering the days.

Some years ago, I had my calendar out and was thinking and praying about some things, and I looked a few years ahead, and then to 2030, then farther into the future, and after a while, I realized, *Whoa, wait a minute... I probably won't be here.* I'm believing to live a while, but that's getting pretty far out. A lifespan of one hundred and fifty years is a stretch. Besides that, I don't want to stay down here after I finish my job. Do you? When my race is run, my course is through, and my tour of duty is done, I ought to be able to leave the

battlefield. Shouldn't I? Go somewhere nice,
somewhere relaxing.

All Phobias Are Fear of Death

I'm believing God is teaching us to renew our
minds and not think wrong, to get absolutely free
from the fear of death. You're not ready and fit to
live until you are ready and unafraid to die. You're
just not. The fear of death affects everything about
your life: you won't do this, you won't step out to
this, you'll do this pensively and with half the
effort, you're always dreading. You're always
wondering, "What if this happens…" There are so
many phobias, and all of the phobias that are on the
list are really one phobia: death. Fear of spiders is
really a fear of dying. Fear of flying is not just that
you are afraid to fly—you're afraid of crashing and
dying. There is a fear of closed-in spaces, of
smothering and dying. You're afraid of heights
because you're afraid of falling and dying. It's a
fear of dying because many believe that dying is the
most serious, worst thing that could ever happen. A
lot of things can happen, but many believe, "When
you're dead, man, you're dead. That's it. Gone.
Done." Wrong! Death is not the end. It is not
termination. It is transition. Death means you leave
here to go there.

The Bible shows some things about how it is
outside of this body, and it is awesome.
We don't realize it, but we are dulled down, way
down. This life on the earth is *slowwwww* and hard

16

and has pressures. Most things down here are heavy
and cumbersome. But then you get out of here, it's
like the lights come on, you're free, and everything
is revealed.

Those who have been "out" and come back describe
the colors and sounds by saying that it's like your
senses are just amplified 1000 times. It's like you
see things you've never seen before, and you hear
things you've never heard before. Why? Because
everything is muted by this flesh and by the sin and
curse that are down here.

There is nothing to fear for the child of God. Death
is nothing to fear. Some might say, "That sounds
good! I think I'll just leave today...." No, no, no.
You have a job to do. Do your job first, and then
you get out of here.

We need mind renewal. When your mind is
renewed and you know the truth, the truth makes
you free. (John 8:32) It will make you free from the
fear of death. When you're free—when you
genuinely have no fear of dying—it turns you into
another person. A person could put a gun in your
face and say, "I'm going to blow your brains out,"
and you would say, "Really? You mean I get to see
Jesus today?" You're not afraid.

"What if this... What if that... What if the other..."
When you're not afraid to die, it gives you a
boldness. It gives you a courage. It gives you a
confidence to live like you're not being curtained,

contained, restricted, and constrained by fear. I'm
not talking about being reckless and stupid, but you
are not being restricted and held in and scared going
out and scared coming back. You will step up, and
you will step out. You will be bold to do whatever
God tells you to do.

They're Not Lost

There are a couple of changes I made in my heart
and mind decades ago, and in how I taught, and
you'll see some of it in this passage.

In Philippians 1:20, he says, "According to my
earnest expectation and my hope, that in nothing I
shall be ashamed, but that with all boldness, as
always, so now also Christ shall be magnified in my
body, whether it be by life, or by death." Did you
know that God can be glorified in your death? In the
way you go? God can be glorified as we live, and
He can be glorified as we leave—in our death.
Verse 21 says, "For to me to live is Christ, and to
die is… *loss?*" People say, "Sorry for your loss…
We lost momma… We lost grandpa… Sorry for
your loss… To die is loss…" Why am I saying this?
Because most of the church world talks "loss" in
connection with death. They do not talk gain; they
talk loss. They say, "I think we're going to lose
them… Yep, we lost them…" Are they lost? We are
talking about believers, now. If you could talk to
them after they died, and you asked them, "Are you
lost?" they would say, "No. I know right where I

am." If you asked, "Have you been lost?" they would reply, "No!"

I don't refer to my loved ones who have gone home to be with the Lord by saying that I lost them, nor do I refer to them in the past tense. Abraham, Isaac, and Jacob are not just people who lived a long, long time ago. They are alive and well today, as are Elijah and Elisha, Peter, James, John, and Paul, right? They're not "were"; they "are." They're just not here; they're there. But they *are* there. We didn't lose them—they just relocated.

If you had relatives in the state of Missouri, and they moved to Arkansas, you wouldn't cry and say, "We lost them. They're over there in Arkansas. We lost them. Sorry for your loss." We didn't lose them. *We* know where they are, and *they* know where they are. Nobody is lost. They're not gone forever; they're just not here; they're there. And we are going to be there too—in about thirty minutes "God time." Maybe an hour. I can wait an hour to see them. A thousand years to God is like yesterday. (2 Peter 3:8/Psalm 90:4) So a hundred years is one-tenth of that, which is 2.4 hours, right? If you've already lived half of your life, if you are sixty years old, then you only have to wait an hour. Can you wait an hour to see your loved ones and your friends? You'll see them in an hour. And to them, that's how it is. I'm convinced: They are with God, so their perspective of time has changed from how it was down here to His time. They're with Him now. So they are experiencing time like He does. I am convinced that people who have been dead for forty years will look up at us when we arrive there and say, "You're already here?" Because to them it was like just a couple of hours. This is Scripture, isn't it?

"To live is Christ and to die is gain." (Philippians 1:21)

"Sorry for your loss... We lost them... They're gone..." Well, they *are* gone from the body and gone from the earth, but *not* gone for good. To die is gain.

He continued, "But if I live in the flesh, this is the fruit of my labour: yet what I shall choose I wot not." (v. 22) You know, the choices we make determine how long we stay here on the earth. Some people leave early, but you don't want to do that. This life is short enough as it is. "For I am in a strait betwixt two, having a desire to depart, and to be with Christ; which is far better." (v. 23) He is saying that he wants to leave and see Christ. Getting out of here and going to be with the Lord is far better than being here—because here, we're walking with Him by faith, but *there*, we see Him face-to-face. (1 Corinthians 13:12)

To die is gain. It would be good to take the word "loss" out of your vocabulary concerning death, and to stop referring to people who have died in the past tense. "You know so-and-so *used to be* this..." "They *were*..." They still *are*. They are very much alive, just in a different place. They are not "used to be." Do you have family and friends who have gone on? They *are*, not *were*. And the next time you see them, they are going to look better than you ever saw them. You never saw your parents and your grandparents when they were eighteen. Just wait until you see them: You're going to be amazed. And as you're being amazed by their appearance, they're going to say, "You don't look so bad yourself." You're going to want to go look in the mirror! We have many issues caused by decay, so we're not at our best right now.

Our Peace Is a Witness

People often say, "Yes, I understand this, but I've lost them, and it hurts and it causes me pain…." Jesus was telling His disciples that He was leaving, and it really bothered them. It upset them. They went to Him one by one and told Him, "No! No! We're going with You. We will die with You. You can't leave us!" He said, "No, I'm going." They were distraught and upset at the thought of not being with Him. But notice what He said to them. In John 14:27, He said, "Peace I leave with you, my peace I give unto you: not as the world giveth, give I unto you. Let not your heart be troubled, neither let it be afraid…" *unless there's a funeral,* or *unless somebody dies*—then you can forget that verse. No! It is such a powerful witness that we are not afraid of death, and that we don't mourn and grieve like those who have no hope when somebody does die. People who don't know these things will look at us and see the strength and light and peace and joy, and they'll say, "How do you do it? How are you not falling apart? How are you not crumbling and just heaving and crying? And how are you not just full of grief and sorrow?" It's because the truth has made you free. The truth has changed your thinking. It has renewed your mind, and you have realized, "Thanks be unto God, He's given me the victory over death. This is not the end. Where is your bite? Where is your sting? Where is your victory, oh grave and death? You don't have it. Jesus has it. He has the keys to death, hell, and the grave. I don't have to be afraid of death." (2 Corinthians 2:14; 1 Corinthians 15:55; Revelation 1:18)

Don't let your heart be troubled. You'll be tempted, but resist it. There will be times when you catch yourself yielding to it, and you will need to stand up and say, "Quit that!" Yes, you'll miss them for a few days, but you're going to see them in forty-five minutes. Can you keep it together for forty-five minutes until you see them again? You didn't lose them forever; they've just relocated.

Rejoice for Them

Notice the very next verse. "Let not your heart be troubled, neither let it be afraid. Ye have heard how I said unto you, I go away and come again unto you. If ye loved me, ye would rejoice, because I said, I go unto the Father." (John 14:28) Friend, if you love them, you rejoice. If you're only thinking about yourself, and you don't have faith in the victory over death, then you'll grieve and sorrow year after year, like there's no hope and like it's the end of everything. But if you love them, and you realize they have no more pain, no more problems, and they are out of here and with the Father, in the presence of Jesus, you will rejoice for them. You will be glad for them, if you love them. Can you see this?

So much of the grieving and sorrowing is just selfishness and unbelief. It's acting like Jesus didn't rise from the dead. It's acting like heaven isn't real. It's acting like all these things are not true.

Oh friend, there is great victory in these verses. There is great victory in this Word. Our thinking can be changed: our perception, the way we talk, the way we act, the way we respond. This is a part of life. This is the way of all the earth. This is happening. In a few more minutes, you and I will be departing this world too.

Receive the Lord

It doesn't scare me. How about you? It doesn't shake me because death is not the worst thing that can happen to a child of God, is it? To depart and be with Christ is gain and far better. (Philippians 1:23) The worst thing that can happen—living or dying— is to be without the Lord. That's the worst thing that can happen to anybody, living or dead. Thank God I'm not without Him. If you've been without Him, you can receive Him right now. You can be with

Him, gloriously born again, with your name written in the Lamb's Book of Life, and with a secure future through death and through to the other side.

The only reason we have this victory is because Jesus died and rose again. The Bible says that He took on a body of flesh and blood, just like us, and He died, so that through His death, He could destroy the one who had the power of death—that is, the devil. (Hebrews 2:14) Jesus did that when He was raised from the dead. He did not need to do it for Himself. He was in heaven and the glory, with the Father. He didn't need it, but *we* needed it. He did it for us. *His* victory over death is *our* victory over death.

Say this out loud:
I have victory in His victory.
The Lord's victory over death, over sin, and over hell is my victory.
It's my victory. I receive it by the blood of the Lamb.

The first step into this journey is giving your life and heart to Him. If you've not done that, you need to do it and not wait one moment.

Say this out loud to affirm or reaffirm your faith:
Father God, I believe in You.
I believe in Your Son Jesus.
I believe He died on the cross and paid for all my sins.
I do believe that You've raised Him

from the dead.
He's alive right now, King of kings and
Lord of lords, soon to come again.
Jesus, I confess You Lord over my life,
Lord over me.
As You help me, I will follow You all my days.
Thank You Lord.

Are you going to number your days? Are you going to start keeping a little better count, maybe, about how much approximate time you have left? Ask yourself, "Am I using it the right way, knowing I'll be out of here really soon?" And people around us are going to be out of here soon, too. But that doesn't have to scare us. It no longer puts us in bondage.

Thanks be to God Who gives us the victory over death through our Lord Jesus Christ. Praise God!

Chapter 2: Never Die

First Corinthians 15:51 says, "Behold, I shew you a mystery; We shall not all sleep, but we shall all be changed." The "sleep" he is referring to is *dying physically*, and not everyone is going to die physically. There will be some who are alive when the Lord comes. But everybody will be changed, whether they've died physically or not. We have to be changed because our body cannot handle what's coming next in its current condition. Mortal cannot inherit immortal, and corruption cannot inherit incorruption, so it has to be changed.

Verse 52 says that it's going to happen "in a moment, in the twinkling of an eye, at the last trump: for the trumpet shall sound, and the dead shall be raised incorruptible, and we shall be changed." Just as sure as you're sitting there, and even more so, the trumpet is going to sound. It's coming. You're going to hear that trumpet.

You might ask, "What if I die?" You're still going to hear it. Everybody is going to hear this one. The dead are going to hear it, and those alive and remaining are going to hear it. That trumpet is going to sound. Verse 53 continues, "For this corruptible must put on incorruption, and this mortal must put on immortality. So when this corruptible shall have put on incorruption, and this mortal shall have put on immortality, then shall be brought to pass the saying that is written, Death is swallowed up in victory." When he says, "Thanks be to God, which

27

gives us the victory through our Lord Jesus Christ," he is talking about victory over what? He's talking about victory over death. This is a reason to shout! He gives us victory over death. Glory to God.

Most Christians don't have a lot of mind renewal concerning these areas. I'm excited about the direction the Lord has taken this because I can sense it will make people free. It will affect every part of our lives.

So many Christians—good people of God, who know they're saved and believe in heaven and in life after death—will cling to their little "flesh" life. They will pay every penny they have, endure every suffering and hardship, and sometimes even compromise their values. They will sacrifice things that they desire and want to do, just to cling to and have another day or two, or another month or two, in this body. That is ridiculous.

People talk about dying like it is the worst possible thing that can ever happen to you. There are many Christians that will hardly go to a hospital or attend a funeral or anything that reminds them of death. It just bothers them. They don't like to think about it. They don't like to be around it. Why? Because they're in bondage. You can't be free until you have no fear. And until you are not afraid to die, you're not free to live. You're not ready to live. That fear and that dread will warp your life.

People say, "I just don't like it. It bothers me." Why does it bother you? Because you're afraid to die? Be honest with yourself.

But good news: You've been given the victory over death, and you don't have to be afraid to die.

Psalm 90:12 in the New Living Translation says, "Teach us to realize the brevity of life, so that we may grow in wisdom."

Find His Plan and Do It!

"Wisdom" has to do with seeing into the future, seeing beyond where I am and where I'm going. It has to do with seeing cause-and-effect, action and result, what's going to happen next. Your life and my life is just like today; it's made up of multiple "todays." Today is partly over, isn't it? If you're going to do something today, you better have a plan, shouldn't you? And you better make some priorities because this day is clicking by.

On a Monday morning, you have a job, and you have things to do. When you get up and get going, you need to have some kind of concept of what you're going to do—what's priority and how you're going to get it done. Why? Because this day is soon going to be gone, and if you don't make it a priority and get on it, you don't have unlimited time to get something done today.

Well, our entire lives are this way. Just like we count the hours and realize, "I'm going to do this...," by that time, it will be four hours later, and by that time, you'll have to do *this*.... You need to see your whole life that way. You need to have kind of a running concept: "Okay, I'm "X" amount of years old now, so even with a long, full life, I'm about this far along, and I need to be on top of what God has me to do in this earth because I am soon and very soon going to be out of here." Numbering our days...

His perspective is accurate. Ours is the one that is skewed. We are slow. The curse and death is in the earth. The planet itself is groaning and slowing and dying. So is your body and everything around you. So time is just creeping. We think it's going fast, but it's not. Think about this: To the Lord, a whole thousand years was like a day. He doesn't perceive time like we do.

They Are In Our Future

Our people—our loved ones and friends that have already gone home to be with the Lord—are with Him, perceiving time as He does. And I'm convinced, if we lived another 50 years, another 75 years, another 100 years, and then we go to be with Him, to those who are already there, it will be like an hour or two. They will look up and say, "You're already here!" We'll say, "Yeah, it was a century...."

This also helps you when you realize you're told not to sorrow like those who have no hope.

Our family and friends are not just in our past; they are in our future.

People get so morbid and so depressed. They say, "I just wanted to have one more meal with momma." Who said you wouldn't get to have another meal with momma? "I just wanted to play ball with Bubba one more time." That's acting like there's no future. It's acting like death is the end, like you have no hope.

As Christians, we know better than this, right? So many things that you wanted to do with them are just goofy things, and when you get to heaven, you won't care. But some of the things you *will* want to do, and you *will* get to do with them. That's not fantasy or fairy tale; that's your future. That's reality.

Do you believe it? If you do, then you don't sorrow like those that have no hope.

Psalm 23:4 says, "Yea, though I walk through the valley of the shadow of death," I won't fear. "I will fear no evil," not any bad thing. Why? Because, "You are with me…"

Psalm 73:23-24 says, *"Nevertheless I am continually with thee: thou hast holden me by my right hand. Thou shalt guide me with thy counsel, and afterward receive me to glory.*"

Psalm 48:14 says, "For this God is our God for ever and ever: he will be our guide even unto death."

These verses say He will be our Guide unto death, and then afterwards, He'll receive us to glory. Didn't He say He will never leave you? He said, "I'll never forsake you." What about when you die? He'll be right there—right there with you. His presence will comfort you. (Psalm 49:15 / Psalm 139:1-12 / Matthew 28:20 / Hebrews 13:5 / 2 Corinthians 5:8)

You'll hear it said that, *"In the end everyone dies alone."* This is never true for a believer. When we reach the end of this life and we breathe our last, He will be right there to take us by the hand and receive us to glory!

God Is Light

An area of interest of mine for years has been the accounts of scores and scores of people's experiences of having died and come back. One thing that impresses me is the similarity of them. Whether they were born in Australia or Africa or Europe or Canada or South America, or if they were thirteen or if they were ninety-five years old, some of the same things happened. You hear people say, "I saw this light. I was above my body looking down, and then I saw this light." I don't know why it took me so long, but I kept hearing about the light, and it dawned on me: **God is Light**. They saw this bright light, and they just wanted to go to the light. The light was so wonderful; it was just pure love. Well, yes—God is Love. God is Light.

You and I are just a little bit away from it, too. Does that scare you? Does it bother you? It should not. "Yea, though I walk through the valley of the shadow of death..." Now if you are in the shadow of something, if you're in my shadow, you are close to me, right? You can't be very far. And if you are in death's shadow, you're about to die. You are right there at death's door. Is it possible that you could be at death's door, knowing you're drawing your last breath, knowing you're dying, and yet you have no fear? Is that possible—that you have absolutely zero fear? Friend, this is the heart of what we believe. The exclamation point of the Gospel is that Jesus was raised from the dead! Hallelujah! Victory over death, isn't it? So you and I should have no fear, absolutely no fear.

Jesus Tasted Death for Us

Now Hebrews 2:9 is very, very significant in our study. Make sure you note this and mark it in your mind and your heart. It says, "We see Jesus, who was made a little lower than the angels," for what purpose? You could say, *so that He could die.* "Crowned with glory and honour; that he by the grace of God should taste," or experience—now this is not sympathy or empathy; He *experienced*, tasted, "death for every man."

Say this out loud: **He tasted death for every man.**

The Bible says that happened by the grace of God. Other translations say that He experienced death for every individual. Why did He do that? What does that mean to us? He didn't need to die for Himself. What does it mean that He tasted death for you and me?

Say this out loud again: **He tasted death for every one of us. Jesus experienced death for me.**

Hebrews 2:14 says, "Forasmuch then as the children," that's you and me, "are partakers of flesh and blood, he," Jesus, "also himself likewise took part of the same; that through death he might destroy him…" Doesn't that make you happy? Destroy him—this is like the devil's *least* favorite verse. He really doesn't like this one. "He might destroy him that had…" What does "had" mean? He used to, did at one time, but not anymore. He "had the power of death, that is, the devil." Oh, the devil hates this verse. He can't stand this verse, because this is the devil's greatest claim to fame throughout his existence: he *was* the "lord of death," he "*had* the power of death," he *was* "lord death…" But he isn't that anymore. He has been stripped. He's been brought to nought. He's been put under our feet. And do you know Who has the keys of death and hell and the grave? It ain't the devil!

Jesus Delivered Us from the Fear of Death

Look at the immediate effect that has on us. In the next verse, what is the result of Him destroying the devil? "And deliver them who through fear of death were all their lifetime subject to bondage." (v. 15) What does the fear of death do to you? It keeps you in slavery your entire life. It will make you tiptoe around *this*, and you won't try *that*, you won't go *there*, you won't do *this*, you'll stay away from *that*, you'll avoid *this*. Why? You think you might have a wreck, or you might get sick, or you might fall, or you might have *this* happen, or *that*—and die! Oh no! Die! *"I'm afraid they/we might die!" "But what if I die? What if I die? Oh no, I may die!"* Actually, if the Lord tarries just a little bit longer, we ARE ALL GOING TO DIE, every one of us.

This bondage is much more pervasive than you might imagine. Don't think that most of the body of Christ is living in this deliverance from the fear of death. Many are living in the fear of death. They're not walking in this freedom. What will the truth do for you? When you know it, you experience and walk in it, and the Truth will make you free.

First John 4:18 is the acid test of what kind of light you have about this. Don't think about someone else—turn the spotlight on yourself right now to see where you are in this. It says, in the Weymouth New Testament, "Love has in it no element of fear; but perfect love," or fully-developed love, "drives away fear, because fear involves pain." Did you see

that? Fear involves pain. The King James Version
says fear involves torment, and other translations
say "torture." Well, that would be pain, wouldn't it?
If you're in torment, you're not in comfort, and
you're not in ease, but you're in pain. If you are
being tortured, you're in pain. If something is
torturing you or tormenting you, you're in bondage.

Now, I love "faith people," and I love "Word
people." They're my bunch. But we've had some
issues in this area. When somebody didn't get their
healing, or somebody died young, or somebody left
in less-than-perfect circumstances, people carry the
torment with them. They believe, "We lost them...
they died young...," and it grieves them. It vexes
them and tortures them. They say, "Maybe we could
have 'stood' better... Maybe we could have prayed
harder... Maybe we could have..." Something is
torturing them. That's not okay. And they're acting
like the person dying is the worst thing that could
ever happen to them. Well, in another thirty minutes
God time, they're going to be gone too. So the
person left eight minutes early—do you really think
10,000 years from now, that's going to be that big
of a deal to us, and we're still going to be talking
about somebody who left eight minutes early?

Yes, we stand, we fight, and we do what we know
to do. We know it's the will of God for us to be
healed, and we know it's the will of God for us to
be delivered, but if you see some people going
early, don't let it torture you. Shout that they are

with Him, and rejoice that you will be, too, in just a little while.

Have No Reverence for Death

There is a reverence for death that has been taught wrongly in churches, and it's contrary to the Scriptures. I know we were admonished as little children when we went to a funeral home, "Shhh... you boys be quiet." When you're a little kid, you're trying to figure all this out because people are standing around talking in hushed tones.

They whisper, "How are you doing?" and the person whispers back, "We're fine."

What are they whispering about? The person is not even there. Some say, "Well, it's out of respect for the family." Okay, you don't want to bother them, but at the same time, reverence for death is an evil thing. It is fear of death. What's really going on is people are in hushed tones because they reverence death. They say, "There's death around here... We need to show respect for the dead..." Do we? What do you mean? You're not talking about showing respect for the dead, you're talking about showing respect for *death*, reverencing death. This should not be. Believers who know their loved ones are with the Lord can stand by the graveside and say what Paul said: "Death! Where is your sting? I don't feel you. I don't even feel your bite, death. Grave! You have no victory!" (1 Corinthians 15:55)

Physical Death Is Not the End

The English dictionary says death is "the end, the end of life, termination, the cessation of all activity and function." You have to study in the Scriptures to see what death is; there's more to it than you see at first. The Bible talks about physical death, it talks about spiritual death, and it talks about the second death. You have to look at the context to see which is being discussed.

But physical death is not the end. Jesus referred to physical death as "sleep." He said, "Lazarus is sleeping. I'm going to go wake Him up." (John 11:11-13)

When Jairus' daughter had died, what did Jesus say? When He went into the house, and the people were groaning and wailing, He said, "Why are you crying like this? She's just asleep. She's not dead; she's asleep." And then they laughed and scorned, knowing she was dead. (Mark 5:39-40) No, this is not soul sleep; this is body sleep.

What is physical death? It's when the spirit departs from the body. It leaves here and goes there, absent from the body, but present with the Lord.

As I mentioned in the previous chapter, I changed the way I talk about this some years ago. I never refer to the death of any of my friends or loved ones as "loss." Fear of death is actually fear of loss. That's what it is. And I don't refer to my friends and loved ones who have gone on in the past tense, because they're not *were*, they're not *used to be*, they *are*. They're just not here; they're *there*. If your relatives moved from Missouri to Arkansas, you wouldn't moan and say, "Oh, we lost them. They're in Arkansas. We lost them!" No, they're just in Arkansas.

Do you believe heaven is as real as Arkansas? It is. And our people are there—and they're occupied, they're ecstatic, and they're free. I said, "They are free!" No more pain. No more sorrow. No more grief. No more curse. No more disease, no more devils, and no more crazy people. None of that. They are totally and completely free. And you and I are finishing up our tour of duty right now. Like I said, most of us have an hour or so left. We can finish our job, and we'll be out of here too. Unless the trumpet sounds before then, and that's good too. We just leave early.

Say this out loud:
> **Thanks be to God Who gives us the victory**
> **through our Lord Jesus Christ.**
> **Victory over death. Glory to God!**

Jesus tasted death for every one of us. What does that mean to us? It would be a very good study to read carefully Romans 5-8 all at one time, and look for what we're talking about. Look for resurrection and victory over death in these chapters. When you read something looking for a specific thing, you see things you haven't seen before. And these chapters are full of this.

We Died With Him

In Romans 6:3, he said, "Know ye not, that so many of us as were baptized into Jesus Christ were baptized into His death?"

We haven't realized the significance of some of the things we've done. When you are baptized in water, and you go under the water, what does that mean? It means, "I died with Him."

Colossians 3:3 says, "For ye are dead, and your life is hid with Christ in God." Actually, other translations say, "You died," "You have died," instead of "You're dead," because you're not physically *dead*, but you did die in Him.

Romans 6:4 continues, "Therefore we are buried with him by baptism into death: that like as Christ was raised up from the dead by the glory of the Father, even so we also should walk in newness of life. For if we have been planted together in the likeness of his death, we shall be also in the likeness of his resurrection: Knowing this, that our old man is crucified with him, that the body of sin might be destroyed, that henceforth we should not serve sin. For he that is dead is freed from sin." (vv. 4-7) He is free from the law of sin and death. Free from the wages of sin, which is death. If you are dead, you can't die. You already *did* die. So now you can't die anymore. You *did* die in Him. Verse 8 says, "If we be dead with Christ…" Are you or not?

Say this out loud: **I am dead with Christ. I *did* die with Him.**

If you did, "We believe that we shall also live with Him." (v. 8) He died, but is He dead? No—He's raised from the dead. Verse 9 is shouting ground: "Knowing that Christ being raised from the dead dieth no more; death hath no more dominion over Him." How does that affect us? He didn't do it for Himself; He didn't need it. He didn't die for Himself. He wasn't raised for Himself. His death was our death. His resurrection is our resurrection. We are in Him, so death no longer has dominion over us. Thank You Lord!

Death has no dominion over Him, and I'm in Him. It has no dominion over me, or over my house, or over our kids, or over our stuff. Death has no dominion over me, so why should I be afraid of it?

Second Corinthians 5:14 says, "For the love of Christ constraineth us; because we thus judge, that if one died for all, then were all dead."

Say this out loud: **I already died in Him.**

Do you know why you don't have to be afraid to die? Because you already did; you already died. If He died for all, then we are all dead. Verse 15 says, "And that he died for all, that they which live should not henceforth live unto themselves, but unto him which died for them, and rose again. Wherefore henceforth know we no man after the flesh: yea, though we have known Christ after the flesh, yet now henceforth know we him no more. Therefore if any man be in Christ, he…" has been born again, "…he is a new creature:" in Christ Jesus, "old things are passed away; behold, all things are become new." (vv. 15-17) Death has no more dominion over Him.

The last part of Hebrews 2:9 says that He "tasted death for every man." He tasted death for you.

Did He take your sins so that you could be in sin? No. Did He take your infirmities so you could be sick? No. Did He bear the chastisement of your peace so you could be oppressed? No. Did He become poor so you could be poor? No. Did He die so you could die? No. This is the same thing: He died, He tasted death, so you wouldn't have to. And if you have faith in Him, then it's counted that you died in Him when He died.

In John 8, the Pharisees, the leaders of the Jews, got so mad at Jesus about the things we're about to read that they were trying to kill Him. They were trying to stone Him. What would make people so mad? Any time you see people that are enraged, you know the devil is behind it. What made the devil so mad that he couldn't stand to hear another word of it, that he tried to kill people just to shut them up? What made him that mad? Resurrection—because he *used to be* the lord of death. He cannot stand resurrection.

No Fear: I'll Never Die

Look at what Jesus said in John 8:51. "Verily, verily, I say unto you, If a man keep my saying, he shall never see death." Is that true? It is. He said that he'll never see death. Oh, that made them so mad. In verse 52, the Jews said, "Now we know that thou hast a devil. Abraham is dead, and the prophets; and thou sayest, If a man keep my saying, he shall never taste of death." How could that possibly be true? Because He tasted death *for* me, I don't have to taste death.

Do you know why I don't have to be afraid to die? Because I never will. I'm quoting the Master; I didn't write this. Is this true or not true? Whether you understand it or not, do you believe that the Master said it? He said you will never die. So why don't you just go ahead and believe it and receive it and say, "I'll never die! I will never die! I will never die!"

This gets even stronger in John 11. Lazarus has died. The body is in the tomb. But in light of what we're reading, was Lazarus actually dead? No, his body was there, but he wasn't. He was out of there, hanging out with Abraham. And Jesus said, "I'm going to go wake him up." And they said, "Lord it's good if he's sleeping. He'll feel better when he gets up." He said, "No, he's dead." He had to say it like that. (vv. 11-14)

It would help us if we would use the right words in talking about these things. If someone asks, *"Where did they bury grandma?"* They didn't bury *grandma.* They buried her body, and the body is just sleeping; it'll rise again. Talking like this would help us to keep our thinking right, wouldn't it? We didn't lose them; they're not gone forever. Their existence has not ceased. It's not termination, it's transition. They just left *here*, and now they're *there*. They're not here with us, but they still exist.

In verse 23, Martha came to Him, and "Jesus saith unto her, Thy brother shall rise again. Martha saith unto him, I know that he shall rise again in the resurrection at the last day. Jesus said unto her, I am the resurrection, and the life: he that believeth in me..." If you believe in Him, then this verse applies directly to you. "He that believeth in me, though he were dead, yet shall he live: and whosoever liveth," that's you, because you believe in Him, "though he were dead, yet shall he live: and whosoever liveth and believeth in me shall never die." (vv. 23-26) You shall never die.

You might ask me, "Brother Keith, are you saying that you're going to live physically on the earth for century after century?" No, no, no. As we read earlier, even if the Lord tarries His coming, and I run my race and finish my course, even if I leave my body, I won't die. And when I'm leaving my body, I won't even taste any death. Even though I leave my body, I will not experience any dying. Why? I died with Him. He tasted death for me. He died in my place, so I wouldn't have to die. Though the body dies, **I** won't die.

Do you remember when they stoned Stephen? The Bible says Stephen called on the Lord and said, "Lord Jesus, receive my spirit." Then he said, "Don't lay this sin to their charge," and he fell asleep. (Acts 7:58-60) Does that sound like some awful, terrible termination? No. I don't think he even knew he died. I'm sure he felt some of those first rocks, but after that, he was out of there, saying, *"Boy, they're pummeling that guy. Oh wait, that's me. But it's not me—I'm here."*

No Fear for the Child of God

Oh friend, we shouldn't think it's some strange, terrible, awful thing when somebody dies. Do you know what *is* awful? Living or dying without Jesus. That's the worst thing that could ever happen to anybody. But for the child of God who knows Him, who loves Him, who is born again, whose name is written in the Lamb's Book of Life, you should have absolutely no fear of dying. You should be looking forward to finishing your tour of duty and getting out of here. If somebody walks up and points a gun at your forehead and says, "I'm going to blow your head off," you ought to say, "Wow! I get to see Jesus today! I thought it would be a little while."

And on your way out, you will not taste one bit of death. You will never die. You will not experience one thing. If your heart stops right now, if your body falls over, if you slip out of it… Of course, like we talked about earlier, two people die every second. So just in the time you read that sentence, two more people died. And two more… somewhere on the planet. Two more. Two more… every second.

In almost every account of a person dying and coming back, the person who died said they were above their body looking down on it. And a lot of times, it took them a minute to even realize whose body it was. I've heard person after person say that even though it was *their* body, it was like they didn't care. They thought, *So what?* They had no connection to it anymore. It's like they were done with it, finished with it.

You step out of your body, and I'm telling you, it will be like somebody just "took the wraps off your head." You're going to see like you've never seen before. You're going to hear and sense things like you've never heard them before. You're going to say, "Whoa! I feel good. I feel like I could run 100 miles per hour. I feel like I could stay up for ninety hours straight."

Your angel will be there, and you'll say, "Hey! Whoa!"

And he will say, "Are you ready?"

And you'll say, "Yeah, man!"

He'll say, "There's some neat stuff in the Milky Way. Do you want me to show you?"

You'll say, "Show me everything! Show me everything!" And you're out of here.

If that is true, and if it is real, why should we grieve and mourn like we've lost them forever? Like it's the end, and like we'll never see them again? That's how unbelievers act and think. Why should we cling to this little "flesh life" like it's the only thing, and in desperation say, "What if they die? What if they die?" Are they saved? Then, it's no big deal for them to die. Fight the best faith fight you know how, but if somebody goes early, don't be tortured, and don't be in torment about it. In a few more minutes, you'll be with them.

Say this out loud:
Thanks be to God Who gives me the victory over death through my Lord Jesus Christ. Hallelujah.

Chapter 3: I Couldn't Tell

The Bible tells us that we ought not sorrow like those who have no hope. The Scriptures also tell us that the fear of death makes us subject to bondage, to slavery. Hebrews 2:14 says, "Forasmuch then as the children are partakers of flesh and blood, he also himself likewise took part of the same..." Jesus had the same kind of body you have. Why? Why did He come and die? As we've already mentioned, the Bible says He tasted death for every man. Why was it necessary to do that? A number of things happened, but here's a big reason: "...that through death," through Him dying, "he might destroy him that had the power of death, that is, the devil." The devil *used to have* the power of death. I know he wants people to think he still does, but he doesn't.

In Revelation, referring to Jesus, it says now He has "the keys of hell and death." (1:18) If you have the keys, you have the control. If I have the keys to the car, you can't drive the car unless you come and see me. I have the keys.

Through His dying and through what He did in His death, burial, resurrection, and ascension, Jesus now has the keys and control, and the devil has been destroyed. The devil wants to make himself out to be some evil, virtually opposite of God, but he's not. He is a fallen, created being who isn't what he used to be. His days are numbered...

Soon and very soon, the Bible says, a great big angel is going to come down with a chain, and he's going to chain him up and throw him into the abyss—and apparently there's not one thing he can do about it. I guess he can't even put up a fight. There's nothing he can do. See, he isn't what he cracks himself up to be. You would think he would at least wrestle a little bit, but nothing. Boom! And I'm not going to shed one tear about that lousy rascal. He's a sorry cuss, and he more than deserves all the punishment he's going to get.

Continue reading in Hebrews 2:15. "And deliver them who through fear of death were all their lifetime subject to bondage." Jesus destroyed him that had the power of death and delivered those who were in bondage.

Fear of death makes you subject to, and liable to, bondage of all kinds. But friend, when you are no longer afraid to die, you are something the devil can't handle. When you are no longer afraid to die, all phobias go out the window, and there will come into your life a boldness and a strength, a courage, and it will change you. You will no longer be bound, restricted, held in, or held down.

This life is the briefest thing we will ever do. It is not all there is. Yet far too many Christians cling to it like this life is all there is, and they will spend anything and do anything just to have another day or two.

You are not going to continue doing what you were doing last week forever and ever. In fact, you're not going to do it much longer. The Bible calls death "the way of all the earth." (Joshua 23:14) So why should we be so shocked when somebody dies? And yet people are. They live in this fantasy world thinking, *I'm going to get up, I'm going to go to work, I'm going to come back, I'm going to wash the clothes, we're going to do this, we're going to get something to eat, we're going to cook, we're going to clean up...* like they're going to do it forever. But how much longer will it really be? Maybe an hour God time? That's reality.

Here's something that will help you. If these things are so, then what about standing by the graveside of a loved one who has just gone home? If we outlive them another 50 years, when we go home to be with the Lord and they see us, they'll say, "Wow! You're already here." Because to them it will seem like they had only been there an hour before we got there. And when you're thinking, *I miss them, and I just can't stand to be without them,* I understand that—you miss them and you'd like to see them— but can't you wait an hour until you see them again? Why should you be grieved and be broken because you can't wait an hour?

If we really have our thinking right in line with the Word, we won't sorrow like the unsaved do. We won't grieve like those who have no hope.

51

Let the Word get in you. Let the Word change your thinking. Don't believe all this junk that's floating around; believe what He told you to believe. Believe the Word. It's true and it's good. It's victory over death.

Say this out loud: **Thanks be unto God Who gives me the victory through my Lord Jesus Christ— victory over death.**

I want us to look at what happens at death. When you're talking about death, it's not as simplistic as some might think. The Bible talks about some people being dead while they live. The Bible talks about being dead in sins. The Bible talks about the second death. So you have to specify what you're talking about. What we're talking about now is physical death. What does that mean? What is physical death? To unbelievers, it is the cessation of life. It is termination. It is the end. That's all, no more. But that's a lie. Saved or unsaved, death isn't the end.

It's Not Me—It's My House

Hold out one hand and touch it with your other hand. This is not you. It's just the house you live in. But it's not *you*.

In the New Testament, when a person is talking about their flesh, they don't refer to it as "me," they refer to it as "the body." I know that sounds like a simple thing, but it will help you so much if you'll change your thinking. It's "the body." It will help you when you're dealing with death.

A while back, a member of my family went home to be with the Lord. We went to the funeral home, picked out the casket, and did those kinds of things. My family was with me in the car, and we stopped and shut down the engine. Before we got out, I said, "Wait just a minute everybody. Wait..." I looked at them all, and referring to our loved one, I said, "She is not here. She is not here." I said it about two more times. "She is not here. What is here? The body. And there's nobody in that body."

Yet, you see Christians weeping and saying, "Where did you put them? Where are they? Where did you bury them?" We didn't. We put that old body over there, but *they* are not there.
It's a shame that this is not real to a lot of Christians. They'll cling to that empty shell, and they'll just grieve and weep and say, "I can't be without you." They will go and sit on top of the grave and hug a tombstone and talk to the gravesite. There's nobody there. Believers should know this, and they don't. Millions of them act just as confused as unbelievers.

Say this out loud: **This body is not me.**

It's not you. What is it? It's the body　the house you live in—but it's not you. If you drive by my house and say, "That's Keith, that's Brother Keith." No, it isn't. "Well, it's his house, you know, it's the

53

same thing." No, it isn't. My house and me are not
the same thing. And right now I'm not in my house.
I'm over here. That doesn't mean I quit existing
because I'm not at my house, right? Many have
gone to gravesides and talked to people as if they
were there. That's like going to a house and trying
to talk to the people who used to live there, but have
relocated somewhere else. If we believe the Bible,
we won't do this.

James 2 describes death. In The Message, James
2:26 says, "The very moment you separate body
and spirit, you end up with a corpse." That's true.
The body is referred to as "a tent, a tabernacle, a
house, a sheath." The Chaldean word is "sheath."
That would be like a holster or like a sheath for a
knife or a sword.

All the other examples parallel this: your spirit and
your body are like a hand in a glove. The glove is
not your hand, but your hand can exist just fine
without a glove, right? But the glove cannot
function without the hand.

People say, "If you never got sick, how would you
die?" Well, if you pull your hand out of the glove,
you don't have to stab the glove to get it to quit
moving, because there's no life in the glove apart
from the hand. And death is just like slipping your
hand out of a glove: You slip out of your body. And
when the body is dead, the body is unoccupied; it is
vacant. Nobody is home. Nobody is there. That's
the truth.

What happens when you die physically? We are given good detail in the Scriptures about what's going to happen. Second Corinthians 4:16 says, "For which cause we faint not; but though our outward man perish...." This outward man is in the process of perishing. Another word for aging is "decay." I know we don't like it, and it's not very nice, but that's what's going on.

The same thing that is happening to your body and to my body is happening to the earth itself. People talk about "saving the planet." It's dying, and ultimately, it cannot be saved. That doesn't mean we have to try to see how quickly we can mess everything up; we may need it for a while. But the Bible says the earth is groaning and travailing. The earthquakes, the volcanoes, the tsunamis, the storms, the tornadoes, the hurricanes—these are groaning and creaking. Why? The earth is getting old, and it's wearing out. It's dying. The bodies that we have came from the earth. The same thing that is in our bodies is what is in the earth.

New Heaven, New Earth, and New Bodies

One of these days, we're going to have a new heaven and a new earth. The new earth is going to be an amazing place. It will never be too hot or too cold or too dry or too damp or too windy. There won't even be any violence in the jungle. The lion will lie down with the lamb and get along and be buddies. Little kids can tie snakes around their neck and not be harmed. And you can run through the woods and never step on a thorn. It's going to be amazing.

All this is here because of the curse that's a result of sin, but our Father is going to make everything perfect again. And we're going to have a body that can keep up with it. He talks about it in these verses.

Continue reading 2 Corinthians 4:16. "Though the outward man perish, yet the inward man is renewed day by day." Inside you are not aging, and you never will. You are developing, but you are never aging inside. You're not any older—as far as aging and decaying on the inside—than the day you were first born again, and you never will be.

Think about your parents. If they have already gone home to be with the Lord, the next time you see them—I'm talking about believers now—you're going to be amazed because you probably never saw them when they were eighteen or nineteen years old. You're going to be amazed at how they look, and you're going to say, "Momma! You look amazing!"

And she'll say, "You don't look bad either."

And you'll say, "Let me see, let me see! Where's a mirror?"

This is not fantasy. This is reality.

Second Corinthians 5:1 says, "For we know that if our earthly house…" What is he talking about? The body. This is not me; it's the earthly house where I live.

The Living Bible calls it "this tent." Well, a tent is a temporary structure. That's exactly what this is. What is my current body? It's my temporary tent. When the Lord returns, He will change the old temporary tent into a heavenly body that will be ours forevermore, made for us by God Himself and not by human hands. We're going to lose this body, but it's going to be changed and become one that's permanent, that will never age, never decay.

Verse 2 in The Living Bible says, "How weary we grow of our present bodies." And we all say, "Amen!" "That is why we look forward eagerly to the day when we shall have heavenly bodies that we shall put on like new clothes." What is this body? It's my temporary tent. It's also my "Earth suit." Just like we were talking about, like a hand in a glove, it's a suit. It's my Earth suit—like when you're out in space, you have to have a space suit. If you don't have a space suit, you can't stay out there, right? And when you lose your Earth suit, you can't stay here. You have to go.

Verse 3 continues, "For we shall not be merely spirits without bodies. These earthly bodies make us groan and sigh…" Have you ever heard it? Groaning? What is that?

Thank God for these bodies now, because if we don't have them, we can't stay. You can't stay down here without this Earth suit. But they always need *something*, don't they?

All the time, they need to be cleaned or brushed or combed or dressed or fed or something. And just about the time you get it fixed or set, you have to start over again, right? All the time. It's enough to make you groan and sigh.

"These earthly bodies make us groan and sigh, but we wouldn't like to think of dying and having no bodies at all." It's not that we want to be bodiless, but, "We want to slip into," something new, "our new bodies so that these dying bodies will, as it were, be swallowed up by everlasting life." (2 Corinthians 5:3-4, TLB)

Mortal Becomes Immortal: It's Just the Beginning...

Death is swallowed up in victory. This mortal is going to become immortal. This corrupt is going to become incorruptible. We're going to be changed, changed, changed. Death is separation from the body; the spirit leaves the body. And like Ecclesiastes says, the body returns to the ground it came from, and the spirit returns to God Who created it. (Ecclesiastes 12:7) Physical death is when the spirit and the body part ways. But it is not the end, by any means, because we will not just remain disembodied spirits. The future is for us to have a glorified, resurrected body that is just like the Lord Jesus' glorified body—that He's in right now. The Bible says it's just like His body.

Second Corinthians 5:5 continues, "This is what God has prepared for us, and as a guarantee he has given us His Holy Spirit." (TLB)

Have you received the Holy Spirit? If you have, then good news: that proves that you're getting a new body; it's a guarantee. Since you have the Spirit right now, it's a done deal, guaranteed!

Verse 6, still reading in the Living Bible, says, "Now we look forward with confidence to our heavenly bodies...." Does that sound like we are dreading dying? It does not. "We look forward with confidence to our heavenly bodies, realizing that every moment we spend in these earthly bodies is time spent away from our eternal home in heaven with Jesus." When we're *here*, we're not *there*. But if you're *there*, you're not *here*. Verse 7 says, "We know these things are true by believing, not by seeing." The King James Version says, "For we walk by faith, not by sight." (v. 7) Verse 8 says, "And we are not afraid but are quite content to die, for then we will be at home with the Lord." (TLB)

What does it mean to die physically? Paul said, referring to his imminent death, "The time of my departure is at hand." (2 Timothy 4:6)

Have you ever been to the airport? They have arrivals and they have departures. If you could stand outside the earth by several hundred thousand miles and see in the spirit, you would see a steady stream of arrivals. I think about 200,000-300,000 a day: births, arrivals. And you would see a constant stream of departures from the planet, like we said, about 150,000-160,000 a day: departures. Arrivals and departures. So when a loved one departs, you don't rip your clothes and grieve like you can't live anymore because they left and went somewhere else. Or do you? No.

People say, "Will we know one another up there?" Only if you knew them down here. Otherwise, you'd have to be introduced and get acquainted, I suppose. Certainly you will know them, because you're going to be *you*. They're going to be *them*, just in a different suit.

When I preached a sermon in church last week, I wore a suit. I was still *me* when I preached the following week wearing another suit. Today you are wearing your "suit." Later on, you'll have another suit, and you'll like it a lot better. But it will still be you—just like it's you right now. It will be a different suit, but the same *you*.

Verse 8 continues, "And we are not afraid but are quite content to die, for then we will be at home with the Lord. So our aim is to please him always in everything we do, whether we are here in this body or away from this body and with him in heaven."

(vv. 8-9, TLB) We want to please Him and to be with Him, whether it's by faith or in person. We're with Him now by faith. We don't see Him, we don't hear Him, and we don't feel Him with our hands, but we know He's here. But it's by faith.

It's going to be great, though, when we actually see Him and actually hear Him. You'll be standing there, and across from you, there's the throne. The angels will be crying, "Holy, holy, holy." This is not a fairy tale; this is real. And in about an hour *(God time)*, you'll be there. Or if you are a younger person, in about an hour and a half or two hours.

What is it like when your spirit slips out of this body? The Bible gives us some very enlightening details.

They Couldn't Tell

In 2 Corinthians 12:2, Paul said, "I knew a man in Christ above fourteen years ago." Many people, scholars, believe that Paul was referring to himself. Whether he was or if it was someone else, the truth is the same. He said, "I knew a man in Christ above fourteen years ago, (whether in the body, I cannot tell; or whether out of the body, I cannot tell: God knoweth)."

He couldn't tell what? Whether he was in his body, or whether he was out of his body, because he had experienced both. But in this particular experience, he says he doesn't know which one it was. "God knows…" And apparently it didn't make a lot of difference to him. "Such an one caught up to the third heaven." The atmosphere above us, from the ground up to seventy, eighty, ninety, one hundred thousand feet—whatever the distance of our atmosphere—that's called heaven: the first heaven; out beyond that: space. But then apparently there's something out beyond that: the third heaven.

Verse 3 says, "And I knew such a man," he says it again, "(whether in the body, or out of the body, I cannot tell…"

Say this out loud: **I couldn't tell.**

He couldn't tell whether he was still in his body or whether he was already out of his body.
Verse 4 continues, "How that he was caught up into paradise…" There is a lot more to heaven than what we have thought. There have been some traditional ideas that I believe will be proven incorrect. The word for *paradise* is like our word for "park," but a "Garden of Eden" type of park. He said he was in this amazing paradise park.

"And heard unspeakable words," he heard words, "which it is not lawful for a man to utter." (v. 4) Some believe that means both "not able to express it," *and* "not allowed to say it." But whether he was in his body there or he was out of his body there, he said he couldn't tell. Why? It must be very much the same: being *in* your body and being *out of* your body. He couldn't tell.

Over the years, I've listened to a lot of people recount cases of dying and leaving their body and coming back. There are some stories you wonder about, but then there are a whole lot of them that are so similar: a teenager from Africa and an eighty-year-old from Canada whose stories sound the same. This one person was a Presbyterian, and this other person had no denomination, or this one was at this place, and this other one was at that place, and again and again—some of the very same experiences.

One man told this account. He was lying on the couch and had a heart attack, and his wife called for an ambulance. He said all at once, he was on top of the house. He thought, *How did I get up here?* He said he saw the ambulance drive up, and he thought, *Who are they coming for?* He said they got out, and they knew that the man had a heart issue, so they brought the equipment they use to give a shock. He said one of the paramedics turned the machine on and then said an expletive, and that it wasn't charged up, so they couldn't use it the way they needed to. He saw them out there—outside his house—with this equipment, then he realized that his body was back there on the couch. It took him a while to realize it. To him, he couldn't tell, I guess. He didn't realize, at the moment, that he was out of his body.

Well, they got him back—revived him—and he told them about the equipment problem. They were amazed that he knew about it. He said, "I saw you. I saw you messing with it."

Up Above Looking Down

Over and over again, you hear the same thing. Usually the person is up above, looking down on their body and the people in the room. In most all of the situations I've heard, they've said that for the first little while, they didn't realize they were out of their body.

One lady's story was really humorous. They had an apparatus hooked up to her to make her immobile, and when they were working on her, something went very wrong, and she died. She didn't know it, but all at once, she was out in the hall, and her first thought was, *Oh! I'm going to be in so much trouble! They told me not to move!* (Because she was out in the hall.)

Now let's stop and notice this: She doesn't even know she's out of her body. Do you see this? She doesn't know that she's dead, because what is "dead"? It's just the spirit coming out of the body.

She said she looked around and heard and saw everything. Then she said there were these lights and speakers, and she was looking at them at her eye level. She remembered from when they rolled her in that these lights and speakers were way up at the top of the room, and she realized, *I shouldn't be able to see this "eye to eye."* She looked down because she was up above everything. She said she looked around the room, and they were all gathered around her body, working feverishly. She thought, *That lady has got problems!* And that was *her* body.

I've heard numerous accounts from people who say that when they realized they were seeing *their* body, and that they were dead and out of their body, it was like they really didn't feel any attachment to that body any longer. It was like they thought, *So what?* They really didn't care about it. It was the old suit.

What is the difference between being in the body and being out of the body? Apparently, initially you won't be able to tell any difference. Paul said, "I couldn't tell. I couldn't tell."

No doubt many of our loved ones who have gone, when they first left, they saw us and heard what we said, if we were in the room or around them. They knew, and then they left. But just because somebody moves to another state, you don't grieve like you've lost them forever.

People grieve and are tormented about it. "I wanted to do this with daddy… I wanted to do this with my brother and sister… I guess I'll never get to do it…" Who said you're never going to get to do it? You're about to see them in an hour, right? Why won't you get to do some things with them? Your loved ones are not just in your past; they're in your future, your very-near future.

Friend, do you believe these things? Does it make a change in your mind, in your thoughts, in the way you hear things and in the way you see things? Is it really possible to stand by the grave and say, "Death! Where is your sting? Grave! Where is your victory? Thanks be unto God who has given us, and gives us, the victory over death, through our Lord Jesus Christ."

Tell the Lord: **I'm not afraid to die, Lord. You're with me always, even to the end. You're with me on this side, and You'll be with me on that side. Thank You Lord.**

It is glorious leaving your body and going home to be with the Lord. But I'm talking about believers, people who have received Him as Lord of their life. If you've *not* done that, then you're not okay. For the one who dies in their sins, dying is a horrible thing, and it *is* to be dreaded and feared. It's only glorious when you *know* that you know your name is in the Lamb's Book of Life and when you know you are in Him. If you've never given your heart and your life to the Lord, friend, now is the time, right now. Don't delay or procrastinate another day. Do it now.

Pray this out loud:
Father God, I believe in You. I believe in Your Son Jesus, and that He died on the cross. He paid the full price for all of my sins. I believe You've raised Him from the dead, and

**I receive You Lord Jesus as Lord of my life.
I believe as You were raised, I will be raised.
Thank You for saving me. Hallelujah!**

Chapter 4: No Longer Afraid

God is going to do something to our bodies so that they will no longer be subject to decay or death. Soon and very soon, you'll never get another wrinkle, never lose another hair, and never have another ache or pain. You won't be subject to that any longer. Age and decay is only for a very brief time down here.

That's hard for us to really understand because from the time we came into the planet, everything around us has been dying. Everything dies: animals, plants, everything—including our own bodies.

But there is soon coming a time when nothing dies. Flowers and trees won't die. You won't die. I know you could shake your head and wonder what it will be like 100 years later, or a thousand years, or one hundred thousand years. It will continue to be perfect and amazing eon after eon.

Did Jesus destroy him that had the power of death? He did. To what effect? To what result? Through destroying him that had the power of death, Jesus "delivered them who through fear of death were all their lifetime subject to bondage." (Hebrews 2:15)

You're Not Free If You're in Fear

Fear of death makes you susceptible to, and accessible by, bondage. You can't be free as long as you fear.

This is a truth you ought to get established in yourself. If you want to really be free, you have to get rid of fear. There's no other option. And what does the fear of dying do to you? It makes you subject to bondage. You cannot be free as long as you fear. And you're not ready to live until you're no longer afraid to die.

That's what the Lord is doing in us in these lessons and with these words: He is making us free. And that puts a courage in you. It puts strength in you.

Hebrews 2:15 in the New Living Translation says, "Only in this way could he set free all who have lived their lives as slaves to the fear of dying."

Did you read that? *Slaves to fear.* Do you want to be a slave to fear? This is why people won't leave their house. This is why people are so apprehensive, and they dread doing *this*, and they dread doing *that*, because they're afraid they might get sick, or they're afraid they might have a wreck, and they instill this fear into their kids.

They tell them, "Don't do that—you'll get killed… Don't do that, you'll die." You need to teach your children to respect what an automobile at seventy miles an hour can do, but you do not want to teach them to fear. People say, "A little fear is good." No, it is not. Reverence of God is good, when it's called "the fear of God." Reverence of God is good, but not fear of death, because fear of death is actually a fear of irrecoverable loss—loss of life, loss of what

I love, loss of what is precious to me, loss of my future, loss.

Their Gain, Not Your Loss

When I hear someone has died, one of the first things I want to know is if they were a believer. Did they know the Lord? Then people say, "Yeah, yeah, I know they were a believer..." Well, then what? Glory to God! Because the Bible says they have gained, not lost. They have gained.

Is there any difference between loss and gain? They are exact opposites. So why should we only talk about loss? And why should all of us contribute to what the enemy is trying to do? At funerals, person after person after person goes by the individual and says, "Sorry for your loss." Loss. Loss. Loss.... And they have to hear it 300 times. Loss. Loss. Loss. Do we need some mind renewal in these areas?

Why should we sorrow like those who have no hope? People do this because they don't really believe what the Bible says; it's not real to them. They're too natural; they're too carnal. This natural flesh and world is more real to them than what the Bible says, than what the Word says.

No, we don't need to focus on their *loss*, we need to focus on their *gain*, don't we? That needs to be our focus, and that needs to be what we talk about. That's what I do every time I go by someone whose

loved one has just gone home to be with the Lord,
especially when I know they are a believer.
Someone might ask, "What if they're <u>not</u>
believers?" They could have become one at the last
minute; it's possible. I believe it happens all the
time. It could happen. You don't know. I believe the
Lord is absolutely merciful. He's so amazingly
merciful and gracious. But especially when I have
confidence that they were believers, that's the first
thing I start talking about.

I was with someone recently, and I went up to them
and said, concerning their loved one, "Well, as soon
as they got there, don't you think—well, you know
they did—they met so-and-so, and they met grandpa
and grandma. They met great, great, great, great,
great, great grandpa, who they had never even
met—and they might just like him, too. And think
about what they're seeing and what they're doing:
They have gain!" They have gained, so why should
we talk about loss?

Hebrews 2:15 in The Living Bible says they "have
been living all their lives as slaves to constant
dread." Dreading.

How many Christians do you think are even right
now—and they may not talk about it every day—
but they are dreading dying. They dread their
relatives dying. They dread it, and they fear it. But
this life is only going to last another hour or so,
right? That's the truth.

First John 4:18 says, "There is no fear in love; but perfect love," and that word *perfect* means "fully-developed love," "casts out," or throws out, "fear: because fear hath torment. He that feareth is not made perfect," or not fully-developed, "in love." And specifically, he's talking about knowing that God loves you.

Are you afraid to die? We're not as strong as we could be, and can be, and *will* be in this. There are many Christians who dread it; they fear it, and they fear their loved ones going. You hear people say, "I couldn't take it if they left... I couldn't live without them..." Don't say that. You may need to.

Are you believing to live a long time? The Bible says, "With long life I'll satisfy you, and show you my salvation." (Psalm 91:16) Do you know what that means? That means you'll be going to a lot of funerals because you're going to outlive a lot of people. If you live a long time, you're going to go to a lot of funerals. And if it tortures you and you can't get over it, if you can't stand to live without them, and you can't deal with it, you're going to have a torturous life. It is just going to keep compounding because people are going to keep dying, and they'll keep leaving.

Look at 1 John 4:18 again. He said, "...because fear hath torment. He that feareth is not made perfect," or not developed enough, "in love." Let me say it like this: not secure enough in God's love for you.

The Weymouth New Testament says, "…fear involves pain."

The New King James Version says, "…fear involves torment."

Verse 18 in The Message says this: "There is no room in love for fear. Well-formed love banishes fear. Since fear is crippling…" What does fear do to your life? It makes you subject to bondage; it cripples you, inside and out. "A fearful life—fear of death, fear of judgment—is one not yet fully formed in love."

Are you afraid to die? Why shouldn't you be afraid to die?

No Fear: He Will Be With Me

I know Who is going to be there when I do: The One Who has carried me from my mother's womb, Who has been with me and walked with me and carried me. He said, "I will never leave you, I will never forsake you," and when it comes time for me to leave this world and slip out of this body, He is going to be right there with me. (Hebrews 13:5)

Again and again, you hear people talk about the light—that amazing light that's just pure love, that is nothing you've ever seen or been into to that degree before. Well, God is light. No wonder people see the light. God is light. Why should we fear that?

Fear has torment. The Weymouth New Testament says fear involves pain. The Message says fear is crippling. You can tell how secure you are in God's love by what is torturing you and what torments you in this life. Fear of death is fear of loss: afraid I might lose my child, afraid I might lose my mother or my brother or my spouse, afraid I might lose my life, afraid I'll lose my future, afraid I'll lose my hopes and dreams. Being afraid is fear of loss, and the fear of loss will torture you. It will cripple you in life, and you'll teach it to your kids. It will cripple them if they don't learn better, and if you don't change. But you can become completely fear-free. You can be completely free of any dread of death.

I Wasn't Afraid

Some years ago, I was first learning how to fly jets, and that was "a different animal," so to speak. Jets are so fast and powerful, and I had been flying a little propeller plane. But I had an opportunity, and this instructor I was with was supposed to be really, really good. He was actually a test pilot, and so I agreed to train with him and did a flight or two, and it went great.

One day I went on a flight with him, and he was going to let me fly. When we got ready to go—and it was at an isolated, independent airport   the guys on the Unicom said to him, "Why don't you do us a trick?" I thought, *Huh? Trick? That doesn't sound good...* And then the instructor replied, "No, I can't.

I got in trouble last time." And I thought, *What? I'm riding home with this guy....* So we got in the plane, and we were ready to go. I was in the driver's seat, and I was going to do the flying. Then they called on the radio again and said, "Be advised—there's nobody around to see. Do a trick," and he said to me, "My airplane." That means "turn loose of the controls and sit back on your hands." I thought, *Okay...* And man, he powered that thing up! We went scooting down the runway and came right off, and I mean, we weren't up a few feet until we shot sharp to the right—ninety degrees, right off the runway. I was gripping the seat, because in order to turn, you have to bank, and we weren't but five or six feet off the ground. If you bank, that means the wing tip gets close to the ground. If you touch the ground, it's usually curtains. I'll put it this way: You're going to need divine help getting out of *that*.

And then all at once, we were ripping right across from where we shouldn't be. And we were low— like at 100 feet, and there were buildings right there. I'm sitting there, and these buildings are just filling up the windshield, and the thought crossed my mind: *You may die right now.* But the thing that blessed me so much was that I realized: *I am not afraid. I am not afraid.* And even though I was in that situation, I thought, *Glory to God! I am not afraid!* I was so happy that I wasn't afraid.

You ask, "What if you crashed right into those buildings and you died?" Well, I would have gotten to see Jesus that day.

Thank the Lord, at the last minute, he pulled out, and we skimmed over the top of those buildings. I think that was the last flight I ever did with him. Because even though you shouldn't be afraid of dying, that doesn't mean you want to throw your life away and waste it.

You hear some people say, "Man, that sounds so good—getting out of here. I think I'll just check myself out today." No, no, no! You are not your own. You've been bought with a price. Your body is not your own to take out when you decide. You've been redeemed; you've been bought and paid for. You need to do what *He* tells you to do. Life is short enough as it is without you cutting it shorter.

First of all, you need to *know* that you *know* that you *know* that you are born again and ready to meet the Lord before you get out of here. This is big.

Second, you need to know that you have run your race, and that you have fulfilled your purpose for being here. The scripture tells us that we are to endure hardness as good soldiers. (2 Timothy 2:3) We are to have a soldier mentality. We're on the front lines here where the curse and the devils and the crazy people are. This is us. We are in the thick of it, and we are to go where we are sent, stay where we're stationed, do our duty, and complete our mission before we get out of here.

If you say, "I don't know what my mission is," you should start finding out because time is passing by. Remember, two more people leave every second.

Another situation happened a couple of years after that airplane incident I mentioned. Phyllis and I were driving in another state down a road that had two lanes going one way and two lanes going the other way, separated by a big median with grass.

We were driving down the road at maybe fifty miles an hour, talking, and all at once, we saw this violent motion, with dirt and grass flying everywhere. Then we saw this vehicle coming at a high rate of speed right over the median, right towards us. I mean, it was just seconds before it was going to hit us head on. You have no time to make a big confession or make a long prayer—it's seconds or less—and I think we both hollered, "Jesus!" You've got time to say that. Which, if that's the last word out of your mouth, it couldn't get much better than that, right? Obviously you believe in Him.

Thank God, at the last minute, that car that was coming right at us, head on, just turned and went off the road. It just turned 90 degrees, and it didn't even touch us. We slowed down, wiped our brow, and thought, *Whew!* And people weren't even hurt. It could have been catastrophic.

But Phyllis and I talked about it later: We weren't scared. We noticed that about ourselves—that we weren't afraid. It was happening so fast—and all of

us are just a breath away from leaving here. Just
that quick, and you're out of here. But we don't
have to be afraid.

Look Ahead

I want you to see why you should have absolutely
no fear. In Revelation 12:11, we see the key to *not*
being afraid. It says, "And they overcame him,"
talking about the devil, "by the blood of the Lamb,"
and something else, "and by the word of their
testimony." See why I'm always "talking and
confessing"? It is key to faith and victory in every
area. And what else does it say? "...and they loved
not their lives unto the death."

Revelation 12:11 in the New International Version
says, "... they did not love their lives so much as to
shrink from death."

The Amplified Bible says, "...they did not love *and*
cling to life even when faced with death..." They
didn't cling to it.

So many people act like this is all there is, and they
cling to this little life desperately. We should not
think that way. We ought to know this is the briefest
thing we'll ever do. This life is just the beginning.
This is faith school. This is when we are being
trained to rule and reign with Him. And He left
some demons and curses and things to practice on—
because if you don't have anything to overcome,

how can you be an overcomer? You have to have something to "come over."

Think about it this way: You have on your helmet of salvation and your breastplate of righteousness, your loins are girded with truth, your feet are shod with the preparation of the gospel of peace, and you're carrying your shield of faith and your sword of the Spirit—what if you're all dressed up and have nobody to fight, and nowhere to go, and nothing to deal with?

So the next time something happens, don't cry, don't whine, don't be a "little whiny-baby." Instead, stir yourself up and say, "Hey! This is just another opportunity to see God move and to have a victory. It's another opportunity to prove my weapons, and the name of Jesus, and faith, and to see God come through again. It's just another opportunity!"

And if it gets really bad, then you need to get "sassy" and say, "Hey devil, make it light on yourself. The worse this gets, and the longer this drags out, it's only going to prove that no matter how hard you tried, you couldn't do it. And I'm going to tell everybody how you couldn't do it."

We're not just conquerors—we are more than conquerors!

My father in the faith, Kenneth Hagin Sr., was born prematurely. He had an incurable heart situation and an incurable blood disease. They told him that if one of these issues didn't kill him, the other would, and that nobody in his condition had lived past sixteen years of age. So sure enough, when he got close to that age, he was bedfast; he was dying. The best doctors said that there was no hope. But God revealed faith to him, and He raised him up off of that bed. Not only was he healed—that's conquering—but he went around for the next sixty years or so and told everybody, all over the world, that the devil couldn't kill him. He told everyone that the devil couldn't do it, and he told them what faith in God would do for them, and how God wants them to be healed. Don't you know that decade after decade, the devil was shaking his head saying, "Man, I wish I would have put that on somebody who would have just laid down and died with it. But no, he had to get healed, and now he won't shut up about it."

That's not just winning—that's making the devil eat it every week until he wishes he had never seen you. That's what I mean by saying, "Hey, make it light on yourself, devil. The longer you drag this out, the worse you make it, and the more you're going to have to eat it."

Isn't it good to know the truth? What does the truth do for you? It makes you free. The truth about dying is that death is not the end, at all. Physical death is separation: the spirit leaves the body. And that's not the end of you or your body, right? You depart and go to be with the Lord.

In John 12:25, Jesus said, "He that loveth his life," what will happen? He "shall lose it." He's talking about *this* life. And remember what we read in Revelation? "They loved not their lives unto the death." (Revelation 12:11) They didn't cling to it desperately.

What did Jesus say when it came time to go? "Father, into Your hands I commit My spirit." (Luke 23:46, AMP)

When Stephen had stones bouncing off of his head, what did he say? "Lord, lay not this sin to their charge." (Acts 7:60) He saw Jesus, and he left there. I don't think that he was aware of the last part of the stoning. He was out of there.

Renewed Perspective

People dread dying. For the believer, though, death is no torment all. But the *fear* of death *is* torment. People dread it—they dread for their loved ones to die, they dread for their parents and grandparents to die, they dread dying themselves. Some say, "Oh, I dread the day… I don't want to think about it… I don't want to talk about it…" Well, you need to talk about it, because it is happening. You need to look at it, and you need to let the truth get in you until you're no longer afraid, and until you are ready— until what the Bible says is true is more real to you than what you see and feel, and until the brevity of *this* life comes into perspective.

"He that loveth his life shall lose it; and he that hateth his life in this world shall keep it unto life eternal." You'll keep it.

John 12:26 continues, "If any man serve me, let him follow me; and where I am, there shall also my servant be." Where is He? He is at the right hand of the Father, where you are going to be. Soon and very soon, that's where I'm going to be.

So why should I cling to this life so desperately? Far too many people are entirely too attached to this life. There is a certain disdain you should have for it. You might ask, "What do you mean?" In the middle part of John 12:25, it says, "...he that hateth his life in this world..." That means when you know the truth, you know that compared to what it's *supposed to be* and compared to what you're *about to experience*, this life here is a drag.

I've heard person after person give their accounts of going and coming back. One of them was saying she saw her dad and hadn't seen him before, because he died when she was a very little girl. When she saw him, she said he looked about 22 years old. She had seen a picture of him when he was that age, but he was old when he died. Well, if decay is no longer an issue, why be old?

For a lot of us, by the time we knew our parents and our grandparents, they were older. But the next time you see them, you're going to say, "Momma! Look at you! You look amazing!"

And they'll say, "Have you looked in the mirror lately?" That's not a fairy tale.

It's okay to have a disdain for this life, compared with what we have coming. It's ok to say, "You know, you get your body clean, and then just a little bit later, you have to clean it again... and the house, when does it ever end... and the clothes, ...and you have to take the trash out again... and it's so laborious; it's such repetition..." It's okay to hate that, to hate this life. Why? Because soon and very soon, you're going to be done with that.

When you think about it, so much of what we have to deal with is because of decay. So much of the dirt and junk and stink and things decaying all around us causes us to have to work, work, work. We put a little pile here, and hide that, and put it in the can, and bag it up, and do this, and wash this away. Why? There's decay; decay is everywhere.

It's okay to say, "Man, I don't like that. I'm looking forward to when we get out of here." But we have a job to do. We are put here for a reason. We have a mission to accomplish, and it's short enough as it is. We need to be redeeming the time, making the most of every day and opportunity. It's clicking by.

Think about this: What if you found out that all you have left down here is the rest of today? What if that was revealed to you? Would it affect what you do today? You might do things differently.

Soon and very soon, there *will* come a day that is your last down here, just like that. Soon and very soon. We must not live like we're going to get up and go to work, go back home, clean the house, go back to work—like it's going to happen forever, because it's not.

This is why we should have zero fear of dying. In John 6:38, Jesus said, "For I came down from heaven, not to do mine own will, but the will of him that sent me."

If you agree, say this out loud: **Me too. That's why I'm here: to do His will.**

Is that true? Then you're not just here to check boxes, to make retirement, to get this done, to get that done, to get comfortable… You were born for a purpose. There's a reason why you're here—now, in this time and in this place. If you don't know what your purpose is, seek God. Fast and pray until you find out what you're supposed to be doing, because soon and very soon, the opportunity is going to be past.

John 6:39 continues, "And this is the Father's will which has sent me, that of all which he hath given me I should lose nothing, but should raise it up again at the last day. And this is the will of him that sent me, that every one which seeth the Son, and believeth on him, may have everlasting life: and I will raise him up at the last day." (vv. 39-40) Is that you? Has He been revealed to you? Do you believe on Him?

We Won't Lose a Thing

Why should I have no fear of death? Because fear of death is fear of loss, and according to this, I'm not going to lose anything. You can't carry your cars and your clothes and your jewelry with you. It's all rusting and rotting anyway. And everything down here is going to melt with fervent heat. But concerning you, and all your life, and your joy, and your good memories, and all your relationships, and especially your future—you're not going to lose anything.

You should have zero fear of dying because fear of dying is fear of loss, and you're going to lose nothing. I'm not going to lose a thing.

People say, "You lost your body." We're picking it up again. Jesus is going to come back and pick it up. I'm not losing a thing. Believers, we're not losing a thing.

When my dad went home to be with the Lord some years ago (and he wasn't that old), there were some things I had wanted to do, and had planned to do—with him and for him. It bothered me the first few days. I thought, *I wanted to do that. I won't get to do that.* I thought that for a few days, and then the Lord spoke to my heart and said, "Who said you won't get to do it?" I thought, *Huh?* See, it was

86

wrong thinking. Can you see that it was tormenting me? It was bugging me. And there was no reason for it to be bugging me—I was just thinking wrong. Preachers can think wrong too, can't they?

I don't mean I heard a voice, but the Lord began to minister this to me. I understood that in time to come, I won't care about a lot of the things I thought we wanted to do. But there will still be some things I *will* still want to do, and we *will* get to do them, together. He said, "Keith, your dad is not just in your past; he's in your future." Is that true?

They're In Our Future

Friend, is this real to you now? In just an hour or an hour and a half *(God time)*, we'll be hugging them. They'll be hugging us. We'll be walking up and down those wonderful, glorious streets, arm-in-arm, hugged up. And they'll say, "Let me show you. You have to come over here. Look at this." Because they've been there an hour or two already, and they've seen some things, and they're going to show us some things. We'll be so excited, and then we can all—you, me, them, Abraham, everybody— get together around the throne of the Almighty God. There will be millions of us in every direction, as far as the eye can see, and when we all lift up our voices in praise and worship… You talk about something you never felt before in your little life down here in the dirt. Oh! And you will never even think about wanting to come back to this life. Oh no.

At the time he was writing Philippians, Paul, you could say, had seen it all. He had been through some things. He had preached to all of the known world. He had been shipwrecked, beaten, and stoned. He had faced-down demons and wild beasts. He had seen miracles. He saw the dead raised and healed. He spent time in jail. And now he's older. In Philippians and in Timothy, he said the time of his departure is here. He's excited about it, and at that point, he said, "I'm wanting to go. I have a desire to go." He was actually wanting to go before he went.

In Philippians 1:20, he said, "According to my earnest expectation... that in nothing I shall be ashamed... Christ shall be magnified in my body, whether it be by life, or by death." Can the Lord be glorified in how you die? Do you think a courageous, fearless death would be a glorious exit? You can smile at your loved ones and say, "See you in an hour or two. I'm out of here. I've run my race. I've finished my course. Y'all work for the Lord and be good now. I'll see you soon."

In verse 21, he says, "For to me to live is Christ," that's what's happening right now, "and to die is gain." Is "to die" loss? Let's quit using the word "loss" all the time concerning people leaving and going. To die is gain. Gain. "But if I live in the flesh, this is the fruit of my labour: yet what I shall choose I wot not. For I am in a strait betwixt two, having a desire to depart..." Is he dreading to go? Is he afraid to go? What is he actually doing? He's *desiring*. He's already done a lot of years of

88

ministry, and he's getting older. He's thinking, *I'd like to go. It would really be great to go.* He has a desire to depart, "and to be with Christ; which is far better." (vv. 21-23) Is that something you dread for yourself or your people, either one?

Some say, "I just couldn't stand it for momma to go. I can't stand the thought of her leaving." They can't stand the thought of her gaining, and of her being far better? They can't stand that thought? They say, "I can't stand the thought of this one or that one leaving... I just can't stand the thought of it..."

Let your mind be renewed. Does it have to be torment because they're going? They are going, you're going, I'm going, your cat is going, your dog is going, your goldfish is going, and your parakeet is going. We're all going. Soon and very soon, we're all going.

But for a child of God, for believers—especially the ones like Paul, who have run their race and finished their course—what about it? It is gain, and it is far better than being here.

When you read the rest of the chapter, you see that Paul decided to stay and help them, and he ministered to them. Then later on, we read in Timothy that he said the time of his departure was at hand: it was finally time to go.

Oftentimes people get ready to go before it's time to go. But you could wait another five or fifteen minutes God-time, right? You can do that. And you will be so glad once you get out of here that you didn't cut it short, and that you didn't fail to do everything you were supposed to do. You'll be glad you stayed and were a good soldier—you held your post, did your duty, and saw this thing through. And then when you leave and you go home, you have nothing to regret. You did everything you were supposed to do.

Was Paul dreading leaving? No, he was desiring to go. You have the same God, you have the same salvation, you have the same Holy Spirit, and you have the same faith. And if you believe that and let it work in you, you will also be fearless when it comes time to go.

Chapter 5: Is Everyone Going to Heaven?

The Lord brought something to my remembrance that I hadn't thought about for a long time. It's an experience that my grandmother had, that she shared with me and with the whole family. She probably shared this experience scores of times, maybe more.

My grandmother, who is in heaven now, was called Sister Lena Pearl by everybody around the house and the community. We're from the South, and in the South, you have good double names. In case something happens to one of the names, you have another really good one right there ready. And they have to have a "flow" to them, kind of a poetic note, like "Billy Bob." All of us had them.

My grandmother, Lena Pearl, was secretary and treasurer of the local Pentecostal church there for decades, and she saw and taught multiple generations. She had dreams and visions, which were much misunderstood. There were people that said unkind things about her because she experienced these things. She was one of the meekest ladies you'd ever want to be around. We used to stay with grandma after school as little kids every day because both my parents worked. In all my time with her, I never heard her use a bad word. I never heard her talk bad about people. Never. Isn't that amazing? She was so meek and humble. The

Lord would show her things sometimes, and she didn't want to tell it, but she would—out of reverence and fear of the Lord. She would stand up trembling and tell things in the church service. And some people would scoff and mock and ridicule. But I saw over the course of decades, person after person who did that come back and repent, when what she said came to pass.

I was at her house one day when a grown man, a big old guy, came and knocked on the door, and he was crying. He came in and knelt at her rocking chair, and he asked her to forgive him for saying and doing the things he did, because what she had seen happened—exactly. It took twenty years because, you know, not everything happens overnight.

She and her mother-in-law, my granddad's mom, were close. I didn't really know her, but they called her Ma Nettie, Ma Nettie Moore. Her husband was Mack Moore. They had twelve kids, and she told all the kids *when* she was going to die, the day. There was talk, asking, "How would she know?" and "I wonder if that's really going to happen." Well, on the day she had told them, she went out early that morning and milked the cow and came back with a pail of milk. When she put her foot on the first step going to the house, she fell dead, with no sickness and no pain. That's the way to go, right? But the kids and grandkids took it hard, and even weeks and months later, they were not doing well.

Well, my grandmother, Lena Pearl, told us this many times, and I would ask her to tell me again.

She said after a long day, she went to the bedroom and laid down at night to go to bed. She said as soon she laid down and her head hit the pillow, she came straight up out of her body and went up, up, up, up. She said she was convinced she went to heaven. She didn't see a whole lot, but she saw this beautiful staircase, that was huge and ornate and—I forget how she described it—but it sounded like it was sweeping. Up at the top stood her mother-in-law, Ma Nettie.

So she went up to her, and I guess they embraced and hugged and rejoiced. She said she didn't look like the last time she saw her. She wasn't old. She was beautiful and so vibrant and young, and she had this beautiful purple gown-type thing on. She said it was almost beyond description. They began to talk, and she said Ma Nettie asked her how everybody was doing since mother had been gone. She told her that they were having trouble getting over this, and that she had been talking with them, and praying with them. Then she asked about my granddad, Lena Pearl's husband. His name was Quinton Nelson, another good double name, and a lot of folks called him "QN."

Now my granddad was not active in the church. He went to church maybe once every year or so, if he had to. If you asked him, "Are you a Christian believer?" He would say, "No." He tolerated my grandmother, and he was a rough guy. He worked in harsh conditions. I saw him rip open his hand and arm, and just cuss and put a rag on it and keep going. He was that kind of guy. He'd drink, smoke, chew, dip, cuss... He was a rough guy, and not a believer.

My grandmother said that Ma Nettie (Quinton's mother) looked at her and said, "Has Quinton changed his way of living since mother has been here?" I can see it right now. My grandmother said she hung her head and said, "No, Miss Nettie. I'll have to say, 'No.'" Ma Nettie said, "Well you tell him if he wants to see mother again, he better change his way of living. Tell him he's got more stock in heaven now since mother is here, and if he wants to see me again, he better change."

Isn't that interesting? Is heaven real? Do you believe heaven is real? Do you believe we have loved ones and friends and family there?

Mothers Want Their Children With Them

The Lord prompted me and helped me to see this— and this is absolutely the truth; I hadn't thought about it like this before. He said, "The most important thing to a mother is the well-being of her child <u>and</u> to be with the child." Right? For every godly mother or believing mother that has gone on to glory, what do you think is the most important thing to them? That every one of their children be with them and with the Lord in glory, in heaven, forever.

Now, QN didn't change the next day, or the next year, or even the next ten or twenty years after that. But my grandmother went home before him, and that hit him hard. A lot of times people don't realize how much spiritual people are holding the family together until they leave. And I'm happy to say that—especially the last 3 to 5 or so years of my granddad's life—he *did* change. He did change. My dad was able to spend a lot of time with him, to pray and talk about the Word. I know he prayed. My dad stayed with him some, and he said he would hear him in the nighttime praying. So we are so glad we can expect to see QN in heaven, too. In a lot of ways, he was a good grandpa. He loved us grandkids. He was just rough around the edges.

Like one fellow said about someone: The guy was a tough rascal until you got to know him—and then he was still tough. That was QN. But that's who Jesus died for, right? All of us that have sinned and come short.

I want to talk about every mother and grandmother getting to see their children again in heaven.

Psalm 90:1 says, "Lord, thou hast been our dwelling place in all generations. Before the mountains were brought forth, or ever thou hadst formed the earth and the world, even from everlasting to everlasting, thou art God." (vv. 1-2)

Isaiah 57:15 says, "For thus saith the high and lofty One that inhabiteth eternity, whose name is Holy..."

What do these words "eternal" and "everlasting" mean? The literal definition is "in perpetuity, perpetual." One of the Hebrew words for these words is interesting. It means "out of sight." How long is it? You can't see that far; it's out of sight. But God is from everlasting to everlasting, which is as far back as it is far forward. That's not something we fully understand or that we will fully understand in this life. The scripture says so.

Ecclesiastes 3:11 says, God "hath made every thing beautiful in his time: also he hath set the world in their heart..." Now, it's easy to read right past this, but this word "world" is actually the word for "eternity." I'm not sure exactly why they translated it this way here, but look at it in the Complete Jewish Bible. "He has made everything suited to its time; also, he has given human beings an awareness of eternity..." He has set eternity in our hearts; we can believe there is eternity, "...but in such a way that they can't fully comprehend, from beginning to end, the things God does." We don't understand much about it.

God is eternal. His things are eternal. What happens past this life is eternal, in perpetuity, without ceasing, without end.

Is Everyone Going to Heaven?

I want to ask a very important question, and I want to answer it from the Scriptures: Is everyone going to heaven when they die?
Now this is a politically-incorrect question, and there are all kinds of people who do *not* believe there is a hell, including some "Christian" people (so-called). I know of certain preachers that preach there is no hell.

But you have *people's* ideas, and you have *the Bible*, right? If you say, "I have a right to my opinions and beliefs," actually, as a believer, you don't. You're supposed to believe what He told you, and not make up stuff as you go along.

What does the Bible say about these things? John 3:15-16 says, "That whosoever believeth in him should not perish, but have eternal life. For God so loved the world, that he gave his only begotten Son, that whosoever believeth in him should not perish, but have everlasting life."

What do we understand *everlasting* to mean? "Unceasing, in perpetuity, without end." We can believe it, but in our present state, we don't understand it. We can believe what we don't understand; it's a choice.

My father in the faith, Kenneth Hagin Sr., used to say that, as a little boy, he could not figure out how a brown cow could eat green grass and give white milk and yellow butter. But while he was trying to figure it out, he was drinking the milk. You can believe and even enjoy something you don't understand at all.

There are many folks who have no idea what happens when they turn the key in their car or when they put it in "D." They have no idea about torque converters, hydraulics, beveled gears, synchro, and universal joints. They say, "Huh?" But you can enjoy the car, and you can get where you're going without understanding it.

Well, you can believe in eternity and not understand what that means.

John 17:2-3 says, "As thou hast given him [Jesus] power over all flesh, that he should give eternal life to as many as thou hast given him. And this is life eternal," this is the definition of eternal life, "...that they might know thee the only true God, and Jesus Christ, whom thou hast sent."

It's not a matter of joining the right church, and it's not a matter of following the exact, correct baptismal formula. It *is* a matter of this: Do you know Him? And if you really do know Him, that shows you've been born again, you have eternal life, you have passed from death unto life, and you love God and people. I didn't say you always acted like you do, but it's in you. It's *in* you.

Everlasting Life or Everlasting Death

Now, when we see these words for *everlasting*, we understand they mean "without ceasing," but I want you to see that the same words are used when describing something else.

Jesus was talking about this in Matthew 25:41. He said, "Then shall he say also unto them on the left hand, Depart from me, ye cursed, into everlasting fire," the same word used when talking about everlasting life. I wonder what it means? "…into everlasting fire, prepared for the devil and his angels." Verse 46 continues, "And these shall go away into everlasting punishment: but the righteous into life eternal." These words are some of the very same words used earlier. If eternal life means "without ceasing," then everlasting punishment means the same thing. They are the same words. Study it for yourself. Does everyone go to heaven when they die? Or is there another place people go?

Daniel 12:2 says, "And many of them that sleep in the dust of the earth shall awake, some to everlasting life, and some to shame and everlasting contempt." *Everlasting* is used in both directions.

In 2 Thessalonians 1:8-9, it says, "In flaming fire taking vengeance on them that know not God, and that obey not the gospel of our Lord Jesus Christ. Who shall be punished with everlasting destruction from the presence of the Lord, and from the glory of his power."

99

Hell Is Real

There are people who say they don't believe there is a hell. And there are people who say, "No, that doesn't mean *everlasting*. They're going to be punished, and then they're just going to be consumed, and it's going to be an end, because a loving God could not do or allow that kind of thing…"

Whether you understand it or not, and whether it suits your version of what's righteous or not, should you believe what the Bible says? Yes, you should believe what the Bible says. I asked the Lord this very question because I knew it would come up. I said, "Lord, what about this? People say, 'How can a God Who is love send someone to an everlasting place of punishment, a hell? How could He do that?'" I asked Him specifically that very question. I said, "Lord, what do I say?" And I didn't get anything specific for a few days.

Then the Lord spoke to me one evening. I don't mean I heard a voice, but inside me. I asked Him again and said, "What do I say about it?" He said, "It's not My choice." I don't know what that does for you, but that went all through me. It's reverberating in my insides even now.

It's Not His Choice

"Why would God send somebody…?" He said it's not His choice. People say, "I just can't believe that.

He's a sovereign God..." Then they need to read some Bible, because over and over, He told people, "I have set before you life and death, blessing and cursing: therefore choose life, that both thou and thy seed may live." (Deuteronomy 30:19) What did He say? *You* choose.

People have not understood how far-reaching this choice goes. He will let you choose even something that will result in your own destruction. He will allow you to do that. It's not His will, and it doesn't please Him, but it's not His choice; it's your choice. And if you don't choose Him, and you don't want Him, where else is there to go? People choose *not* to be with Him. Where are they going to go?

Is there a hell? A lot of people today don't believe that, even some churchgoing people. I don't know what they do with all of these scripture verses, but they don't believe them, and they've formulated their own theories, opinions, and doctrines. There needs to be a standard, not "every man does what's right in his own eyes," and not what you think or what I think. There has to be a standard. Do you know why a lot of people say they don't believe in hell? Because they don't *want to* believe in hell. Just because you don't *want to* believe it doesn't mean it isn't there. And you don't want to wait until you're out of here to find out how stupid you were, right?

Isn't it great that we all have an opportunity right now, right here, when we're alive and we're breathing? Do you want to go see momma in heaven? Alright, then let's do it.

In Luke 16:19-20, Jesus said, "There was a certain rich man, which was clothed in purple and fine linen, and fared sumptuously every day: And there was a certain beggar named Lazarus," a *certain* beggar.

Now there are people who try to say, "Well, this passage is a parable. Jesus is speaking allegorically." No way is this a parable. Jesus *did* teach in parables, and every time He did, He would say, "Such and such is like unto such and such..." You don't see that anywhere in this, and when you're talking parables, you don't give the typical people specific names. There was a *certain* person, and it was a certain person named Lazarus. If I said there was a man who lived in Branson named Dave Smith, would you say, "He's telling a fairy tale; that's a parable"? No. When you use specific names, and when you say "certain," then it happened. This happened, and it gives us a window to see some things that happened past this life after death, and to see some people that don't go to heaven.

"There was a certain beggar named Lazarus, which was laid at his gate, full of sores, and desiring to be fed with the crumbs which fell from the rich man's table: moreover the dogs came and licked his sores." (vv. 20-21) He had a hard life. Verse 22 continues, "And it came to pass, that the beggar died, and was carried by the angels into Abraham's bosom..."

Now think about it: Lazarus' body is in the ground, but he's being carried somewhere. This life is not all there is. This body is just the house you live in right now. And at death, you'll leave this body. Where will you go?

Well, Lazarus was carried by angels into Abraham's bosom. "The rich man also died, and was buried; and in hell he lift up his eyes, being in torments," there is a hell, "and seeth Abraham afar off, and Lazarus in his bosom. And he cried and said, Father Abraham, have mercy on me, and send Lazarus, that he may dip the tip of his finger in water, and cool my tongue; for I am tormented in this flame." (vv. 22-24) There is a hell; there are flames. There is torment, right? And you'll see through this passage, he keeps talking about torment, torment. He keeps on referring to torment...

"But Abraham said, Son, remember that thou in thy lifetime receivedst thy good things, and likewise Lazarus evil things: but now he is comforted, and you are tormented." (v. 25) There's a place of comfort, and there's a place of torment after this life. "And beside all this, between us and you there is a great gulf fixed: so that they which would pass from hence to you cannot; neither can they pass to us, that would come from there." (v. 26) He said, "We can't. I can't come to you. I can't do anything for you."

Why would God send a man to a place like that? It wasn't His choice. But if you won't choose God, if you don't want to be with Him, if you don't want to believe in Him, if you won't accept Jesus, if you don't want to accept the salvation and redemption He has provided for us, then you have to go somewhere else.

Verse 27 continues, "Then he said, I pray thee therefore, father, that," if you can't come help me, "thou wouldest send him to my father's house…" that's what we've been talking about. What do people who are past this life want for their loved ones? For their sons and their daughters? For their grandchildren? What would they want most of all? They don't want them going to the place of torment. They <u>do</u> want them going to the place of comfort.

He said, "Send him to my father's house, for I have five brethren; that he may testify unto them, lest they also come into this place of torment." (v. 28)

Where is hell? What is it? It's real. I believe the Bible. Do you? If Jesus said there's a hell, then there's a hell. If He said people go to it, then they do. I know people don't like to believe it, and they have changed it into all kinds of things, but I believe the Bible. How about you?

Choose Today

One of the scriptures we talked about says, "Choose you this day whom you will serve," and Joshua went on to say, "As for me and my house, we will serve the Lord." (Joshua 24:15) Whose choice is it? It's not God's choice; it's our choice.

We are told that hell is beneath us, and heaven is above us; there are scriptures that talk about this. Isaiah 14:9 says, "Hell from beneath is moved for thee to meet thee at thy coming: it stirreth up the dead for thee..."

The Bible talks about the heart of the earth–that's the Latin word for "core." There's something at the core of the earth. We already know one thing about the core: it is hot. How hot is it? Well, nobody has ever actually been there with a thermometer, but it is estimated to be somewhere around 10,000 to 13,000 degrees. Some conjecture it can be as hot as the surface of the Sun. Natural things reflect spiritual things.

There are people there beneath us, spirits. It's a place of torment. Jesus talked about people being cast into hell fire in Mark 9:48, "Where their worm dieth not, and the fire is not quenched." The same word "everlasting" refers to the "fire never going out," and "worms not dying." It's everlasting.

What is the most important thing you need to decide about hell? "I'm not going!" Nobody should go to hell.

Every mother and grandmother and great-grandmother that is in heaven should get to see their

105

kids and grandkids and great grandkids. A real "Mother's Day" is when Bubba and Sissy and the whole bunch joins momma and Jesus, right?

What decides who goes where? Well, we've already talked about it. We have a choice.

The truth will make you free. You can play "ostrich," stick your head in the sand, and pretend these things are not real. You can kid yourself and say, "Well, maybe later on, right before I die, I'll give my heart to Jesus." What if you get caught off guard? What if you don't have time or your mind and heart is not in the right place? You have today. You have right now. Do you think you ought to take advantage of what you have right now? You're alive, you're breathing, and you have a choice.

I recommend that you read the last three chapters in the Book of Revelation. They are so powerful, and they give you a telescopic vision into the future. It's not fantasy or imagination. The Lord let John see what is going to happen and how everything is going to work. It describes heaven, and it isn't fantasy—he actually saw it. It's real. You're going to see it—as a believer. Even if you live another fifty years or one hundred years, it's going to go by quickly, and you're going to see it. The next thing you know, you're going to be saying, "Wow! Look at that! Do you see that? Look at this!"

Heaven Is Amazing

Heaven is amazing, and it's a place of comfort. It's a place of love. It's a place that doesn't even need a light bulb or a sun, because the light of God—Who is love and light—lights it all the time. You never have a nighttime. What kind of place, what kind of world, what kind of life? It's amazing. It's wonderful. Everybody ought to go.

I'm going. How about you? I've made up my mind. I made my choice. I'm going. I'm not going to hell. It wasn't made for me. It was made for the devil, his crowd, and people who don't want God. I do want God. I want Him now and forever; I want to be with Him.

How can we know that we are not going to hell and that we're going to be with Him?

In Revelation 20:1-2, John said, "I saw an angel come down from heaven, having the key of the bottomless pit and a great chain in his hand. And he laid hold on the dragon, that old serpent, which is the Devil, and Satan, and bound him a thousand years." There is a hell, and there is a devil. The Bible says so very plainly.

Now, forget about anything you ever saw or heard on a Hollywood movie about demons and devils. It's a bunch of junk. Don't you believe all that fantasy. That's not what it's like. It's real, but it's not like that.

"And cast him into the bottomless pit, and shut him up, and set a seal upon him, that he should deceive the nations no more, till the thousand years should be fulfilled: and after that he must be loosed a little season." (v. 3)

In verse 6 he said, "Blessed and holy is he that has part in the first resurrection: on such the second death has no power." You'll see from this passage that there are two resurrections; there are two deaths. He said for those that have part of the first resurrection, the second death has no power over them. "But they shall be priests of God and of Christ, and shall reign with him a thousand years." That's me.

Verse 7 continues, "And when the thousand years are expired, Satan shall be loosed out of his prison," and do you know what he does after 1000 years of cooling his heels and thinking about it? The very same thing he always did: lie, steal, and kill; that dirty-dog rascal. But it's his last "hurrah."

"And the devil that deceived them was cast into the lake of fire and brimstone." There is something beyond hell, after hell. It's called the lake of fire, "…where the beast and the false prophet are, and shall be tormented day and night for ever and ever." For how long? These are the same words that described everlasting life: for ever and ever. (v. 10)

"And I saw a great white throne, and him that sat on it…" There is a great white throne, and there is One

Who sits on it. It is the Judge of all the earth, the Creator of the heavens and the earth. It is the Almighty. We're going to see Him. And when you do, you will not be disappointed. "...from whose face the earth and the heaven fled away; and there was found no place for them." (v. 11) The Lord has to bring a new heaven and a new earth.

Verse 12 says, "And I saw the dead, small and great, stand before God." Obviously it wasn't the end of them when they died here on the earth because he's looking at them—everybody, from the least to the greatest, known and unknown. "...and the books were opened: and another book was opened, which is the book of life: and the dead were judged out of those things which were written in the books, according to their works." Does it matter what you do and don't do in this life? It does and it will, after this life. Verse 13 continues, "And the sea gave up the dead which were in it; and death and hell delivered up the dead which were in them: and they were judged every man according to their works. And death and hell were cast into the lake of fire. This is the second death. And whosoever was not found written in the book of life was cast into the lake of fire." (vv. 13-15)

The Lamb's Book of Life

Who is *not* going to the place of torment? Those found written in the Book of Life, that's who. Anybody not found written in the Book of Life is going to the place of torment, and eventually to the lake of fire. I know folks don't like to believe it, but I believe the Bible. How about you? If you really don't like the idea, I have the solution: Make sure your name is in the Lamb's Book of Life.

You ask, "Do I have anything to do with it?" It's absolutely your choice and no one else's.

Revelation 3:5 says, "He that overcometh, the same shall be clothed in white raiment; and I will not blot out his name out of the book of life, but I will confess his name before my Father, and before his angels." Whose name is in the Lamb's Book of Life? The same one that Jesus confesses before the Father. We also have words that Jesus said about this in other places, including Matthew 10:32. Jesus said, "Whosoever therefore shall confess me before men, him will I confess also before my Father which is in heaven." Who is in the Lamb's Book of Life? The ones that Jesus confesses before the Father, the ones who confessed Him here, in front of men. This is right here in the Bible.

Matthew 10:33 says, "But whosoever shall deny me before men, him will I also deny before My Father which is in heaven." If you won't confess Him, if you're ashamed... Another account says, "If you're ashamed of me and My words before this evil and adulterous generation..." (Mark 8:38) It's not okay to be a "closet" Christian. Do you want the Lord to stand up and confess you and claim you in that day that we just read about—when heaven and earth will flee away from the face of the Almighty, and the only people *not* going into the lake of fire are those whose names are written in the Lamb's Book of Life? Do you want to *know* that you *know* that your name is in that Book and that He is confessing your name? How would you know that would be so? Because you boldly, without reservation, unashamedly, confess Him before men. You believe in Him and are not ashamed.

He said if you do that, "If you confess Me before men, I will confess you before the Father and His angels." Revelation says those are the ones whose names are written in the Lamb's Book of Life.

Jesus had sent the disciples to cast out devils and heal the sick, and they came back and said, "Jesus! Jesus! Even the devils are subject to us in Your name." (Luke 10:17)

Do you know what He replied? He told them, That's great, but let Me tell you what you ought to be happy about: that your names are written in heaven. (Luke 10:20)

As great as miracles, spectacular things, and victories can be down here, they pale in comparison to this great truth: When your name is written in the Lamb's Book of Life, you are forever a citizen of heaven. You are forever a part of the family of God, sons of the living God, that rule and reign with Him forever. It's not a theory, it's not an opinion, it's the Bible. Do you believe it? It is the truth. Hallelujah!

Chapter 6: Do Yourself No Harm

I'm very excited about this chapter. I believe a number of lives will be lengthened, spared, and changed because of this word, and that people will get the strength and victory they need to overcome.

I want to talk about something that is a bit sobering, but it is needful. When you know the truth, it sets you free. There's victory in it. We've talked in detail about what happens when you die. There have been many people who have died and come back. The next thing they knew they were up above their body looking down on it. Some have said at first they didn't even realize it was their body. I heard one person say, "Wow, I didn't realize I looked so old." And Paul said concerning his experience, "Whether in the body or out of the body, I could not tell." (2 Corinthians 12:2-4)

So you may be out of your body for a little while before you realize, *I just died*. And yet, you're not dead. It's not even the end of your body. The Bible says that the Lord is going to come back, the trumpet is going to sound, and your body is going to be raised. He is going to perfect it for you and give it back to you. **But death is not the end**. When godless people talk about death, they say, "You know, it's just blackness and nothingness; you're gone, and that's it, the end, period." It is not the end. The Bible reveals that unbelievers depart and go down, to a place of torment. But Christians depart and go to be with the Lord, which the Bible says is far better than being here. To the believer, it's not loss; it's gain.

I remember one lady who said she was having surgery and died. She didn't realize it, but she had died, and she was above her body looking down on the operating room. Later, she described to the surgeons what they did and what they said—and they were in shock.

They said, "No way," because at one point, they were talking about some things that weren't surgery-related, and she told them what they said. They were shocked. Then she told them about a problem they had had with a piece of the equipment, and they knew for sure that there was no way she could know that.

She was out of her body, and she described what she saw. She said, "You can't describe the colors. You have never seen color this vivid, and you've never heard like you do there." It's as though all the plastic and junk is taken off of you, and you can really see and really hear. You have never felt so wonderful. It's never been so amazing. Person after person after person says that they saw the light— that bright, bright, amazing light that was pure love—and they just knew, *I have to go there...*

It took me a while after listening to this to realize, *Well, of course: God is Light.* He is. If it's so wonderful like that—and I'm convinced it is—then why not just check out now? Just leave this place of tears? I'm talking about suicide. Why not just take your own life and get out of it?

This has happened far too many times with people. Most everyone either knows someone or knows of someone who has been affected by suicide. It has hit them hard and caused numerous vacuums and holes in their life, as well as pain and loss. I want to talk about it. If it's so much better for the child of God to be "out of here," then why not just leave early? Why not just quit? Why not just go? Well, there are several reasons why "not," and very good ones. **I want to give you 3 big reasons why you should not take your own life.**

REASON #1
The devil is lying to you about the hopelessness of your situation.

I was disturbed to read that the third leading cause of death for young people between age 15 and 24 is suicide. That doesn't have to be. It's sad. Why does a person take his own life, and what happens when he does?

Again and again, it's connected to despair, depression, hopelessness, and pain. People have come to believe, "It will never be any better. There's no hope, and there's no reason for me to stay." Or, people come to believe, "I'm hurting, and I just want it to stop." They view it as a way of escape. But what happens when you die or if you kill yourself? Is that the end? Is that "lights out"?

115

No. If you kill yourself, you're going to come out of your body, and you're going to get a close-up look at what you just did.

I heard one lady describe it—and it is rare to hear this—but she became despondent and hung herself and died. She said that as soon as she was aware she was out of her body, she regretted it. She deeply regretted doing it. You know, it's different once you get out of the flesh and all the junk that's around you. You see clearly. Thank God one of her friends came in and found her, lifted her up, used life-saving techniques, and she was revived. That's why she is telling her story, obviously; they got her back.

She was so thankful—you could hear it in her voice and see it in her eyes. She has helped numerous people *not* to commit suicide. But why does it happen? Why has it happened so many times? People get in pain, and the devil is a liar. He's mean, and he's cruel.

I remember being 13, and what it's like to experience your first heartbreak. It's awful. You've never experienced anything like that before: you fall in love—at least what you know about falling in love—then somebody doesn't return your affection or feelings, or they decide they found a better deal somewhere else, so they just drop you like last week's trash. It hurts. It's a hurt that you've never experienced before, and at that point of vulnerability, the devil will come and say, "This is an unbearable pain. Nobody has ever hurt like you're hurting." That's a lie. Pretty much everyone has... The truth is, it's never as bad as the devil makes it out to be.

The Bible says, "There hath no temptation taken you but such as is common to man." (1 Corinthians 10:13) Everything you're experiencing has been experienced by people all over the world. But the devil is very tricky, and if you'll listen to him, he is trying to convince you, "This pain is an unbearable pain. What you're dealing with is hopeless. Nobody knows, nobody can relate, and there's no point in going on." Sometimes in these moments of weakness and desperation, a person does something they can't take back.

Now what I want you to see in the Word, as we progress, is that if people would just give God some time, they could see miracles. If you have been around a little while like I have been, and if you've made it past age 10, 11, 12, 13, and you've made it through some things, you have a different perspective now. We now know that even though it hurts so bad, it isn't the end of the world. Just give God some time, and, like I say, "Go have an ice cream and take a nap." If you'll just give God some time, you can see miracles.

Say this out loud: **Things can change very quickly.**

I believe that lives will be spared and lengthened, and that these words will find people's hearts. The devil's devices will be revealed, and people will see what's going on—and they won't yield to suicide.

In Acts 16:26, Paul and Silas had been beaten and imprisoned. Even though they weren't physically feeling wonderful, the Bible says they prayed and sang praises to God, in the dark, smelly, dungeon. If things are bad, do you have to get depressed and get down? You can be strong and praise God in the midst of the worst stuff, can't you? They were doing it.

As they were praising God, it says, "Suddenly there was a great earthquake, so that the foundations of the prison were shaken: and immediately all the doors were opened, and every one's bands were loosed." Now that's a very specific type of earthquake. Verse 27 says, "And the keeper of the prison awaking out of his sleep, and seeing the prison doors are open, he drew out his sword, and would have killed himself, supposing that the prisoners had been fled." Was he right? No. I wonder how many other people have made assumptions and killed themselves, when it wasn't even true.

Did you know that Job was suicidal at one point—if you want to call it that? In the third chapter of Job, he kept saying, "Why? Why did this happen? Why didn't this happen? Why?" He kept saying, "Why? Why?"

You have to watch out for that. When you start thinking it and verbalizing it, that's an indicator that you're listening to the devil, and you're going down a wrong, dark path. If you keep talking about what you don't have, and what hasn't happened, and what you can't do, and what they didn't do, that's negative, and there's death in it. You get to the point where you're not thankful for all the things you do have and for everything that God has done for you and is doing for you. You get to the place where you can't see anything but death and dark and problems, and that's when the enemy will suggest, "That's the only way out. It's too bad, and it will never be any better. There will never be any hope. You can never get back to as good as what it used to be." What did we say? *Give God some time.* Give Him some time to help you. Don't take it out of His hands.

The keeper of the prison was ready to kill himself. This was the equivalent to taking a pistol and putting it to your head. They didn't have pistols; they had swords. So he has this sword up against his chest, or his body, and he is about to gut himself. He's about to kill himself—to cut his throat or whatever with the blade—and in verse 28, it says, "Paul cried with a loud voice, saying, Do thyself no harm…"

Is there a word in the Bible for those contemplating suicide? Is there a word for those who think it's helpless and hopeless, and nothing can be done, and it's the only way out? The Lord says, "Do yourself no harm." Don't hurt yourself. Did God say, "Don't hurt yourself"? He said it through Paul. He said it by the Holy Spirit and had it recorded in the Word for all generations. Don't hurt yourself. Do you think that would include doing things like cutting yourself, abusing yourself, and doing things that you know are destroying parts of your body?

Say this out loud: **<u>Don't hurt yourself.</u>**

He said, "Do thyself no harm: for we are all here." He was about to shove his sword inside his body when he heard, "We're all here," and he thinks, *What?* It was almost too late.

The devil is a liar. He'll tell people, "Nobody cares about you." That is a lie. "You're not doing anybody any good; you're just causing everybody problems. Everyone would be better off without you." Lies. "You're just a big mess up. You've never done anything right in your life." Lies.

Let's analyze this statement: "You've never done anything right your whole life." Maybe you sweetened the tea just right one time. Maybe you took the trash out exactly right. There is no way that you "never did anything right." You trimmed your eyebrows perfectly. There has to be *something* you did right in your life.

Why am I saying that? Because the devil is such a liar, and when you get in this negative *I've never done anything but mess up* thinking, it's a lie. You know it's a lie, so why are you repeating a lie? "Nobody cares about me." You know that's not true. They might not be happy with all of the things you've been doing, but it doesn't mean they don't love you.

Here's the truth: You are a one-of-a-kind masterpiece, made in the image and likeness of God. The next time the devil says, "You're not worth anything," ask him, "Then how come Jesus paid so much to get me?" God is no fool. He doesn't pay a billion dollars for a twenty-five cent item. He wouldn't do it. He paid the biggest price that's ever been paid for anything in the universe for you and me. Don't you believe the devil's lies. Don't you sit or lay in the bed and cry, feeling sorry for yourself. "Nobody cares. Nothing's ever right, and I don't have a future. Nothing's ever going to happen for me." How do you know? You've only been alive for a very short time.

So how much do you know about anything? Have some faith in your good God, and give Him some time to show you something. Give Him some time to help you, get you out, and show you what He can do.

Look at the prison guard's situation. The guy has the sword up against his chest or his throat, whatever it was, and he's just about to ram it, thinking, *There's no hope. They'll execute me in the morning anyway, so there's no reason for me to stay around here. Everybody's gone. I'm dead*

121

anyway. I'm a dead man. Isn't that how the devil talks? "You're a dead man anyway, dead to everybody." No. When you hear that negative talk, it's the devil. Don't believe it, don't listen to it, and don't yield to it.

What did Paul do? He said, "Don't do yourself any harm; we're all here." The guard replied, "You are?" and threw the sword down. "You're here?" It was pitch dark in there. Verses 29-30 say, "Then he called for a light, and sprang in, and came trembling, and fell down before Paul and Silas, and brought them out, and said, Sirs, what must I do to be saved?" What if he had just been two seconds quicker on plunging that sword into his chest?

Verse 31 continues, "They said, believe on the Lord Jesus Christ, and thou shalt be saved, and thy house." What if he had plunged the sword? What about his family? "They spake unto him the word of the Lord, and to all that were in his house. And he took them the same hour of the night, and washed their stripes; and was baptized, he and all his, straightway. And when he had brought them into his house, he set meat before them, and rejoiced, believing in God with all his house." (Acts 16:31-34)

A couple of hours earlier, he essentially had the pistol to his head with the hammer cocked. Just a few hours later, he was sitting there laughing with the man of God, with all of his family saved and loving God and free. Look at what he would have missed if he had taken his life in that moment of desperation, if he had believed lies that the prisoners were all gone, that there was no hope, and that he would be executed anyway.

Can you see what's going on? The devil is so subtle and so deceptive. He is such a liar. What do we have to do in these situations when it looks hopeless, and the pain seems unbearable? ***Give God some time.***

Psalm 91:14 in the God's Word translation says, "Because you love me, I will rescue you." Do you believe that you can count on the Lord when He said, "I will rescue you"? He said, "I will protect you because you know my name. When you call to me, I will answer you. I will be with you when you are in trouble. I will save you and honor you. I will satisfy you with a long life. I will show you how I will save you." (vv. 14-16) He's not going to leave us and forsake us. If you'll just give Him some time, do you believe He will do this? "I'll be with you. I'll rescue you. I'll help you. I'll protect you. Let me show you how I can save you. Give Me an opportunity. Give Me some time. Let me show you." Glory to God.

Why shouldn't you just check out and take your own life? Because it's never how it seems and feels. It's never as bad as the devil makes it out to be. He is lying to you, trying to deceive you in order to destroy you. But it's not the end. It's not hopeless.

Here's something else you need to know. In Acts 20:22-23, Paul said by the Spirit, "And now, behold, I go bound in the spirit to Jerusalem, not knowing the things that shall befall me there: Save that the Holy Spirit witnesseth in every city, saying that bonds and afflictions abide me."

Did Paul have some challenges in his life? Did he have what you might call some "low points," when he was really tried and tested? Yes, Paul had his moments—moments when he despaired of life—but he made it through, and we're going to see how he did. He said on this occasion, "I know bonds and afflictions are waiting on me there." The Spirit of God had shown him. But did Paul say, "*Well, my free life is behind me, my best days are behind me, and all I have to look forward to is beatings and jail. To depart and be with Christ is far better than being here.*" No. What did Paul say? **<u>But none of these things move me.</u>** You ought to put that phrase in your arsenal. When you feel your lowest and your most stressed, what do you say? "None of these things move me."

The devil is trying to move you to despondency, despair, hopelessness, and helplessness, and to make you think you are an utter victim. But he's wrong. You're a victor. You're an overcomer. You're more than a conqueror. You have victory over death itself. In verse 24, Paul says, "None of these things move me, neither count I my life dear unto myself." I'm not desperately clinging on to these few days in this life; this is not all there is.

"So that I might finish my course with joy," not a last gasp of desperation. "Finish it with joy" because the joy of the Lord is your strength, "and the ministry, which I have received of the Lord Jesus, to testify the gospel of the grace of God."

REASON #2
We all have a God-ordained course that we are supposed to follow and complete. We're not supposed to stop halfway down the course. We're supposed to find and finish our course.

Say this out loud: **I have a course to finish.**

Sadly, many Christians have just wandered all over the place and done everything under the sun *except* try to find out what they're supposed to be doing. But if you're alive, it's not too late to find your course. There's something you're supposed to be doing. There are things in which you're supposed to be involved. You are supposed to be connected with and helping other people. And you're not supposed to quit until you finish your course.

Now you'll be tempted to quit, but doesn't the Bible talk about running your race with patience and perseverance? It is important. There's a lot of work to be done, and everybody needs to be doing their job. If you leave early, and you don't do your work, guess what? We have to do it. Don't be surprised if you do that, and later on, we show up at your house in heaven and say, "Hey, what was the idea leaving early and not getting your work done? We had to do yours and ours too." I'm sure we'll forgive you and get past it, but you may hear from us about it.

Now some people say, "Well, aren't people who commit suicide lost?" I don't know why you'd think so automatically. If you were saved before you committed suicide, why wouldn't you be saved after? If you were lost when you committed suicide, you'd still be lost after.

People have all these ideas about it: "Well, technically, yes, but if you did this, and you were already dead, could you get forgiveness?" That's just men's reasoning and thinking. If you're saved before you did it, you're saved after. And you know, why would killing yourself be that much different from killing somebody else? That's not an unpardonable sin. It's not an unforgiveable sin. It's a sin, and it's wrong, but there's no need to assume that because a person committed suicide, he is automatically going to hell or that he is lost. I see no reason to assume such a thing. If you're saved before, you're saved after.

Like this woman who attempted suicide by hanging described, she wasn't saying she was *lost*. She said that she regretted it immediately. It hit her, and she was sorry. She was so glad she got an opportunity that most people don't get—to come back and get it right.

In 2 Corinthians 1:8, Paul said, "For we would not, brethren, have you ignorant of our trouble which came to us in Asia, that we were pressed out of measure, above strength, insomuch that we despaired even of life." Paul was having some moments, wasn't he? He said, "We despaired of life." What does that mean? He didn't want to keep living. He didn't want to keep going. This is Paul we're talking about.

I don't care who you are, how much you think you know, or how much you think you know about God—you can be pressed beyond your limit. You can be pressed to the point where it just seems you can't handle it—and you actually *can't.* I know a lot of people think, *Well, I'm strong. I can handle anything.* But the truth is anyone can be maxed out and pushed to the point where they are tempted to despair of life. Anybody. And if you think not, then you've just never been pressed that far.

But we need to learn what Paul learned because he didn't quit. Verse 9 says, "But we had the sentence of death in ourselves, that we should not trust in ourselves, but in God which raiseth the dead." This is victory over death, isn't it? The devil will come and say, "You can't handle this. This is too much for you. You're not able to overcome it. You're not able to deal with this." A lot of times, you need to look up and say, "You know, you're right. I can't. I'm not enough, but I'm not alone. I have Somebody with me, and 'greater is He that's in me than he that is in the world.'" (1 John 4:4)

There was a time when Paul pressed the Lord about helping him concerning that thing that was oppressing and vexing him, and what did the Lord tell him? "My grace is sufficient for you." When he got the revelation, he said, "When I'm weak, that's when I'm strong. When I get to the place where I have no more, that's when I tap into the Almighty; that's when something comes up inside me that's beyond me." (2 Corinthians 12:9-10)

You'll notice when people get ready to commit suicide, they keep saying things like, "I can't. I can't handle this. I can't do this. I can't go on." No believer should talk like this when the scripture says, "**I can** do all things through Christ who strengthens me." (Philippians 4:13) Don't say, "I can't." Maybe in yourself you can't, but through Him, Christ Jesus Who strengthens you, you can.

Paul went on to say in 2 Corinthians 1:9-10, "We had the sentence of death in ourselves, that we should not trust in ourselves, but in God which raiseth the dead: Who delivered us…" This sounds like the 91st Psalm, doesn't it? Did He deliver Paul? Was He with him? Did He protect him? Did He rescue him, help him, and honor him? "He delivered us from so great a death, and he doth deliver: in whom we trust that he will yet deliver us." Don't you like this? He delivered us. He delivers us. And from anything that happens in the future, He *will* deliver us. We're going to make it. We're not going to quit, we're not going to give up, and we're not going to say, "It's hopeless. We're helpless victims." No, we're not. When I'm weak, that's when I'll be strong. God will come up in me. His Spirit will quicken me. He will help me.

If you despair and pull the trigger or swallow the bottle of pills, then you take it out of God's hands and don't give Him any opportunity or time. You have no idea what you missed, or what you might have been able to do to help others in time to come. Friend, your victory is also other people's victory. When you overcome, it affects lives around you. Did you know that? But if you give up and quit, that will affect lives around you, too. You would not want to give up and quit and inspire three other people to commit suicide over the next ten years. They look at you and think, *Well, if they couldn't make it, I can't either, so I might as well check out too.*

You don't want to be that kind of inspiration. You want to be the inspiration of the man or woman who—no matter what—wouldn't quit. You held on to God, and He turned the situation around and showed you how He could save. Then year after year, when people ask you about it, you can stand up and say, "It never gets too bad for God to help you out. He will help you out of anything. I know I felt like it, but He brought me out. I'm so glad I didn't quit, because now I'm enjoying this, and I've been a part of that, and these last ten years we've had this... Now I'm not just going in empty-handed. I have some fruit. I will have some rewards in the next life."

I'm not quitting, how about you? I'm going to run
my race, and I'm going to finish my course. That's
what Paul said in 2 Timothy 4, years after all these
ordeals had transpired. Paul had been shipwrecked,
beaten, stoned, and betrayed. He went through some
things, didn't he? But in 2 Timothy 4:5, he's telling
Timothy, the young minister under him, "Watch
thou in all things, endure afflictions, do the work of
an evangelist, make full proof of thy ministry."
Then in verse 6 he says, "I am now ready to be
offered, and the time of my departure is at hand."
They are boarding right now, and my flight is about
to leave. He continues, "I have fought a good fight,
I have finished my course, I have kept the faith."
Glory to God. "Henceforth there is laid up for me a
crown of righteousness, which the Lord, the
righteous judge, shall give me at that day: and not to
me only, but unto all them that love his appearing."
(4:5-8) Would that be us?

Now God is a faith God. "Without faith it is
impossible to please Him." (Hebrews 11:6) Is it
"faith" if in desperation you quit, give up, don't try
anymore, and you succumb? Or when you say, "I'm
defeated, it's too late, it's over"? As soon as you get
out of the body, guess who you're going to see. Is
He going to be pleased with you that you quit and
didn't try? No. What pleases Him? Faith pleases
Him.

This is so much better than being cut off in midlife,
robbing yourself of the remainder of your years. If
you have another 50 or 75 years to go, it will pass

by quickly, like telephone poles on the highway when you are going a hundred miles an hour. The next thing you know, you're going to look up, and it's going to be time to go anyway. Why cut it short? These days are precious days that we have. Our time on earth is very precious. Isn't it so much better to stick it out through the pain, the anguish, the desperation, and the temptations to say, "No. I don't care. God has helped me before. He'll help me this time. He'll never leave me, and He'll never forsake me. I'm not going to take my own life. I'm not going to quit. I'm not going to give up. I'm going to give Him time to help me and show me."

And then you make it, and it gets better and better. You get free, and then something good happens. Then something even better than that happens. There are challenges, but you overcome them, too. There are tests, and it hurts, but you don't quit. Then something else good happens, and the next thing you know, you get up one morning and realize, "Glory to God. I'm done. The time of my departure is at hand, and I can honestly say, 'I'm finished. I don't feel like there is more I have to do. I have fought a good fight. I have run a good race. I have finished. I'm about to reach out and hit the ribbon. I'm finishing my race.'"

The next thing you know, you're out of your body, and when you meet Him, He will say, "Well, done; good job. You were faithful in a few things. I'm going to make you ruler over much. You didn't quit; you stayed with Me." (Matthew 25:21) All the pain and anguish of the earth will be like something that happened in three seconds, and you'll never think about it anymore. You'll have eternity to enjoy the fruits of your reward.

I want you to say this to see how it feels:
I have fought a good fight.
I finished my course.
I kept the faith, and I'm ready to go.

Isn't that the way to do it, after you've seen it all and done it all, and you're old? You're so old that the old people call you "old." Then you're out of here.

Why shouldn't you just end it? Why shouldn't you just take your own life? There are lots of reasons why, aren't there? The devil is a liar. It's never as hopeless as it seems to be, if you just give God time. You are on a course that you're supposed to finish. You need to do it. You need to go all the way.

Finally, why should you *not* commit suicide? Why should you *not* take your own life?

REASON #3
You are not your own.

In 1 Corinthians 6:19-20 in the Easy to Read Version, it says, "You should know that your body is a temple for the Holy Spirit that you received from God and that lives in you. You don't own yourselves. God paid a very high price to make you his. So honor God with your body."

Are you going to strangle it? Are you going to blow a hole in its head with a 44-Magnum? Are you going to take a bunch of pills? Are you going to cut its wrists? Whose body is it that you could be destroying? Whose is it? You might say, "Well, it's my body." Is it? Actually, it's been bought and paid for with a very high price, and before you do anything to it, you need to go to the Owner and tell Him that you're thinking about doing this to His body, and see what He says about it. Do you think He is ever going to give you permission to blow a hole in the head of His body? Or cut its wrists or any such thing? No. He's going to tell you, "No. Don't you dare do that to My body. I bought it. I paid for it. I'll heal it. I'll help it. I'll resurrect it. I'll transform it." But no, you don't have a right to do just anything that crosses your mind with it; it's not yours. It's His.

Don't you think that the phrase when He said, "Do yourself no harm," would also include not cutting yourself, defacing yourself, maiming yourself, or hurting yourself with large quantities of drugs or other kinds of things that you know are damaging and hurting you?

It's not just your body—it's His. Do you believe it? So let's take care of His body and do what He says to do with it. Sanctify it to His service. If it's sanctified to His service, He has an obligation to maintain it. Did you know that? I count on that. I say, "Lord, now this body is in Your service. I'm counting on You to keep it up and keep it working until I run my whole race and finish my course." I say it frequently, "This body will serve me well as long as I need it." It will serve me well. God will keep it that way. You are not your own.

Before you leave this world, there are some vitally important things you need to do. Death is not the end. What we do in this life affects the next life.

First, are you born again? Please do not leave this place unsaved, dying in your sins. You need to know that you are saved and right with God. Second, have you finished your course? Do you know that you've done everything you're supposed to do? And third, realize you are not your own.

SALVATION PRAYER:

Father God, I believe in You.
I believe in your Son Jesus.
That He went to the cross and paid for all my sins and failures.
That You have raised Him from the dead.
Jesus, I receive You and all You have done for me.
I confess You as Lord of my life.
I am not my own, but I belong to You.
As You help me, I will follow and serve You all my days.

If you have contemplated suicide or you've attempted suicide, and you see the truth, just repent before the Lord. Nobody else has to hear it. Close your eyes and look up toward the Lord in your heart. Just tell Him, "Lord, I'm sorry. I repent for listening to the devil's lies. I repent for yielding to hopelessness and helplessness. You are greater than all. Nothing is too hard for You."

Say this out loud:
By the grace of God, I will not quit.
By His strength in me, I won't give up.
When my strength is gone, and when I'm not
enough, You are with me.
Your grace is sufficient for me.
And when I can't in myself, I can do all things
through Christ Who strengthens me.
As You help me, I will fight the good fight.
I will finish my course.
I will keep the faith.
Hallelujah.

Chapter 7: Heavenly Minded

Many of us are over halfway finished with our assignment down here, and we're soon going to leave. This life down here is the roughest thing we'll ever do; the roughest part is happening right now. After this, it's just "joy unspeakable and full of glory." We can make it a few more days down here. The Lord is helping us. We can finish our assignment. We can run our race.

Do not leave this world in your sins and without Jesus. There is something worse than this life: hell. We've talked about it.

Often when folks have a family member with a sickness or a disease, they start to think that it could happen to them, too, and they get into dread. People don't want to go to hospitals or be around funerals. Why? When someone talks about dying, people say, "Oh, don't talk about that..." The Bible says dread and fear make you susceptible to being in bondage. We should be completely fearless about dying, and ready to go.

I'm reminded of a story. Years ago, a couple of guys who had been hunting were walking down a dirt road carrying their shotguns, and they met some other folks, strangers. These guys' pastor had been encouraging them about being evangelistic—and being bold—so they were going to try it out with these strangers. They stopped and asked them, "Do you want to go to heaven?" The folks looked at them and their weapons and said, "No." So they said, "No? You mean you don't want to go to heaven when you die?" They said, "Oh, sure, when we die. We thought you were getting up a load right now."

Life Here Is Brief

The Bible tells us to pray, "Lord, teach us how brief our time is and to number our days." (Psalm 90:12) We need to live with that awareness. Some years ago, I'd seen some things that were just tragic and really heart-wrenching. I just sat down in my chair and asked the Lord, "God, the love I have is from You, and nobody cares more or loves more than You." I said, "How do You tolerate this evil and pain and suffering in the earth? It bothers *me*. How do *You* tolerate it?" And just like that, He answered me—and I can't describe the tone, but it was love. He said, "Son, it's very brief." He's telling me how *He* tolerates it.

From His perspective, even if it was 30 years of suffering, just like that, it's done. The redemptive plan is available to anybody who will lay hold of it. But are you ready to go? Because soon and very soon, we're out of here.

What happens when we die? It's not an unknown. The Bible tells us what happens. Ecclesiastes 12:7 says, "Then shall the dust return to the earth as it was," our bodies are made out of it, "and the spirit shall return unto God who gave it."

When you die physically, your spirit leaves your body. James says that a body without the spirit is dead. (2:26) It's compared, in the Chaldean language, to pulling a sword out of a sheath. When your spirit comes out of your body, it's like pulling a hand out of a glove. Brother Hagin said that when he was a teenage boy, he died and then came back, and he described it. He said, "It's just like putting your boot on in the morning." He said that he went back in his body through his mouth. The same word *spirit* is translated "breath." And, of course, when you die, there's no more breath. Why? Because the spirit is gone.

When people die and come back, over and over again, you hear them describe the same thing. The person says all at once they were above, looking down on their body. A lot of times, they're hearing and seeing people around them, and it takes a little while for them to realize what's happening. I've heard several of them say they looked at their body and thought, *Look at that poor dear. Boy, they need some help.* It took them a while to realize that it was *their* body. But then they said they didn't care. They were glad they weren't there.

Their senses—sight, sound, and everything—were just off the chart compared to being in this body. This is a dull veil. We're seeing everything blurry. Because of this flesh, we're hearing and perceiving everything "dulled down" and "dumbed down."

When you leave here, it's going to be like you took off your blinders, opened up your hearing, and all of your senses are just going to go, "Whoosh." We're going to see colors we never saw. We're going to hear sounds we never heard. We're going to experience sensations we never experienced.

With Christ Is Far Better

The Bible says, "To be absent from the body is to be present with the Lord, and to depart and be with Christ is far better and gain." (2 Corinthians 5:8; Philippians 1:21) It is gain. People say, "I'm sorry for your loss..." when people die. Well, if they were a believer, you didn't lose them. People say, "Well, where did you bury them?" You didn't. They're not there. That's their body, but *they* are not there. Where are they? They're not in the casket. When you die, you go up or you go down; you don't hang around.

People ask, "What about people haunting places?" No, human spirits don't just get to hang around on the earth after they leave their body. A lot of times, if there is some kind of spiritual phenomenon, there are evil spirits that are impersonating people— spirits that are "familiar" with individuals, who know things about them.

That's one of the reasons the Lord told us not to seek soothsayers and fortunetellers, because you just open yourself up to be deceived and duped. People say, "It was real; it was spiritual." I don't doubt that, but that doesn't mean it was God. The devil can do some things, too. You do not need to call a number and have your stars read or your palm read. You're just opening yourself up to be deceived by the enemy, so do not do it. You don't need that; you have the real thing. You have the Holy Spirit. He's real, and anything you need to know, He'll help you and show you.

You depart and go to be with the Lord. That's what happens. You slip out of your body, and you go to be with Him. Colossians 3:1 says, "If you then be risen with Christ, seek those things which are above, where Christ sits on the right hand of God."

Now there's no doubt where He's talking about. This is the Heaven of Heavens, where God is. Jesus is sitting on the right hand of God. We have more than one description of that throne. Ezekiel saw it. John saw it—he recorded it in Revelation. He described how it looked like sapphire and how there was a sea in front of it and a rainbow round about it. Part of it looked like emerald, and God looked like fire. Some descriptions say "like glowing metal." He didn't see His face necessarily, but he saw His form sitting on the throne. And then there were the winged creatures. Brother Hagin said he saw them one time. He said that they're strange looking, that they have eyes that go all the way around their head, and they're looking in every direction at once. We've never seen anything like that, have we? They're real.

Set Your Heart on Heaven

The Bible tells us we're to seek the things there. Verse 2 says, "Set your affection on things above, not on things on the earth." The Good News Translation says it like this in verse one: "You have been raised to life with Christ, so set your hearts on the things that are in heaven…" (Colossians 3:1)

Say this out loud: **"Set your heart on the things that are in heaven."**

He's very specific about the heaven he's talking about—where Christ is sitting on His throne at the right side of God. You and I are supposed to think about that and be mindful of that, to set our heart on that while we're living here. Verse 2 says, "Set your affection on things above, not on things on the earth."

Have we been doing that? Most people have not. In fact, there's kind of this unspoken belief that we're really not supposed to think too much about heaven, and that God hasn't really told us much of anything because He didn't want us to know much of anything. Then you hear people say phrases like, "Well, you know you don't want to be so heavenly-minded that you're no earthly good."

Well, what they're talking about is being goofy-minded, thinking about some kind of fantasy. That's not going to profit anybody. But actually, being heavenly-minded helps you live right here on the earth. Our Jesus is there in heaven. Our Father is there. Our relatives are there. Our friends are there. Our mansion is there. Our property is there. Our citizenship is there…

Living down here is the briefest thing we'll ever do. We are truly just passing through. It's the truth. I know it seems like a while because this is the only thing we've ever done so far. When the Lord calls us His *little children*, it's not a figure of speech. We really are little children. I don't care if you're a hundred years old; you are God's little one. You're just getting started in this, and out past this life is when it really starts getting interesting.

This is training time. God is teaching us how to trust Him and live by faith, how to follow Him and obey Him. All of the things we're learning, and all of our spiritual development, we will take into the next part. The Bible says, "Your works will follow you." (Revelation 14:13) What you have done will go with you. It says that you will have possessions there.

In Hebrews 10:34, he said to them, "[You] took joyfully the spoiling of your goods." They had some of their stuff taken from them, and they took it with joy. How could you take it with joy when people are taking away your car, your house, your stuff, your clothes, your jewelry? Because you know that you have—in heaven—better stuff and lasting stuff. They didn't get your *good* china; they can't get your *good* stuff. Didn't the Bible say that if you give to the Lord, you give to His people? When you give to the poor, you lay treasure in heaven where moth can't corrupt it, and where thieves can't steal it. (Matthew 6:20)

Say this out loud: **"My good stuff is up there."**

So if something happens to your stuff down here, do not fall off your chair. Don't sweat it. It's all just temporary. Everything down here is like a gallon of milk. What do I mean? It has a date on it, and it isn't lasting long. It's just good to use for a little while, and then everything down here, as the Bible says, will perish. "The elements shall melt with fervent heat." (2 Peter 3:10) Everything. There's not going to be anything down here saved. Nothing. There's going to be a new heaven and a new earth.

You Can't Take It With You

Years ago, when I was teaching at Rhema, I overheard some of the students having a conversation. It was the beginning of the year, and one of them—who was supposed to be "testifying"—was really just bragging about all of the things he had. It was a little annoying and irritating. A couple of the others were listening and kind of started shuffling their feet, trying to be polite. Finally, one young man just piped up and said, "Well, so what? Your pile of ashes will be bigger than mine!"

You aren't taking it with you. Nobody brought anything into this world, and nobody is taking anything out—as far as natural, physical things. But your works *do* go with you—your spiritual works and your spiritual development. The Bible says you have possessions there, as we just read. (Matthew 6:20-21)

There actually are some things that *were* on the earth and are in heaven now, one of which is the Ark of the Covenant. John said in Revelation that during his experience, he saw it. At one time, it was down here. The priests were hauling it around, and God said, "That's mine. I want it up here." Heaven is real, and everything that has been prepared for us, the Bible tells us, is what we should be thinking about. Where your treasure is, that's where your heart will be. (Matthew 6:21)

We should not live down here like this is everything—like our possessions or our retirement is everything, and that it is going to make us happy forever. You're not going to be here but about another 30 minutes in "God time." Thank God for some nice things that we can use and get our needs met. We're thankful for that, and especially for things we can use to love and bless and help other people. It's good, but it's very, very temporary. But you have things in heaven. You have permanent stuff.

There was a man who fell from a height and hit his head on the sidewalk, and he died. When responders got to him, he had no pulse, no anything. But they worked on him, and after several attempts, they finally got him back. He told them when he got back that he had gone to heaven. What does the Bible say? When you die, you depart and go to be with Christ, if you're a believer. (Philippians 1:23)

We'll Have a Place

He told them, "I saw my place." They said, "You saw your place? What do you mean?" He said, "Man, I have real estate." People have this idea that in heaven, there are little, white cookie-cutter structures, maybe with some columns in the front. He said, "I had a lake. I had a mountain behind my house. It's everything I ever wanted." And he said, "I saw the Lord, and I said, 'Lord, this is just amazing. How did you know? I didn't even know I liked that. How did you know?'" Then he said the Lord looked at him and smiled and said, "I know what each of my children like, and I custom build their abodes for them."

That word *abode* is the actual word that is used in John when He said, "I go to prepare a place for you. In my Father's house there are many mansions." (John 14:2) That word is *abode*. One word it's related to is *manor*. A "manor" is a landed estate, and I don't think they're all going to be cookie-cutter houses, because we don't all like the same thing, do we? I wonder what your place is like. They're working on it right now...

What did Jesus say? "If it wasn't so, I would have told you. I'm going to prepare a place for you, and I am coming back for you. Where I am, you are going to live with Me. You're going to stay with Me." (John 14:2-3) This is not a fairy tale. I wonder what your place looks like. I wonder what's there. You will have stuff.

Brother Jesse Duplantis tells of an experience he had of going to heaven. He described it. He said the Lord let him see his house, and he said when he went into the foyer, it was just everything that he would ever desire. He said he had some pieces of furniture in his house that were similar to some he had down here. But he said there was one piece in the foyer like nothing he had ever seen before. He asked the angel that was with him, "Where did that come from?" The angel said, "The great Lord God knew you would like it; it's from Him."

Can you imagine? You're going into your place, and you have somebody over to visit. They say, "Now that is a chair! Where did you get that chair?" And you fold your hands and say, "The Father gave me that chair." The Father. He sent some of my angels over here, and they said, "The Father wants you to have this chair."

Say this out loud: **"I have a place. I have stuff. My citizenship is in heaven."**

Philippians 3:20 says, "Our citizenship is in heaven." (NIV) Glory to God. Take a moment to thank God that He loves us like this, and that He has done so much for us. Thank You Lord.

There has been a misconception that we're not supposed to know about any of that, and we're really not supposed to think about it. That is not true. That's contrary to verses we've already read. The Bible tells us that we ought to have our mind on it. We ought to be thinking about it. Why? Because if all you do is live for the here and now, you're going to live a carnal life. Instead, see this life as temporary, and that it is not the main thing you should rush after and desire. The Bible says if we have this hope in us, this glorious hope of Jesus' return and of Him taking us with Him, it purifies us. (Titus 2:12-14; 1 John 3:3) You'll live differently when your focus is there instead of here. It will help you live right and holy and pure.

So are we supposed to be thinking about heaven all the time? Are we supposed to be mindful of things above, not of things on the earth? He said it very specifically. It's the truth, so let's do it; let's make the adjustments.

Say this out loud:
**Lord, I pray, from now on, remind me to set my heart and my mind
where You are in heaven, where my things are in heaven,
and where my future is with You.**

Why should we be so focused on *here*, when we're not here for that much longer? We should be thinking about where we're *going*.

My Dad Overcame

On May 21, 2005, my Dad went home to be with the Lord. The way it happened troubled me, but the Lord ministered to me. I was really close to my Dad. He was a buddy to me and my brother. He taught me how to fight. He taught me how to eat ice cream. He taught me how to get rubber in second gear in a Mustang, how to pop a wheelie on a motorcycle, and how to shoot firearms. You know, important stuff.

Our family had some good times—my brother and I, him and Mom. My Mom and Dad were very supportive of us in the ministry from the beginning, from the very beginning. Thank God I didn't have some of the struggles a lot of people have. Even though other folks might have thought I lost it, *they* didn't. Even if they didn't understand, they stayed hooked and believed in us, and they prayed for us. They saw the start of the Branson church and some other things.

We were able to take them with us to a meeting we were going to have down in Florida. They were going to be with us for that week, so he and Mom and myself were flying there in a small plane.

149

Now my Dad had had a real fear of flying, and he
didn't like it. So I didn't push it for years. You
know, flying was a part of my life, but he just
wasn't comfortable with it. But he was not the kind
of guy to just let something whip him. He said this
thing was not going to beat him, and he wasn't
going to miss out on things like meetings because of
a fear. So he told me he was going to go. And I
thought, *Well, ok.* So we went.

On the way down there, as we were flying—
actually very close to where the Sarasota church is
today—at several thousand feet, he died. I'm flying,
and he's in the back, and it seemed like it took half
a day to get that plane down on the ground and
landed to meet the ambulance. But I had to focus on
flying the plane, and he was gone.

The next few weeks, three weeks actually, it
troubled me; it bothered me. He was only 68 years
old, and I thought, *God, you know there were things
I wanted to do, and we wanted to do, and we had
plans. We didn't have to do that flight. Did I miss
You? Should I have said, "No, don't do it, don't
go"?* All those kinds of thoughts and feelings.

I cried, I prayed, I was troubled, I was vexed. I was
confident he was in heaven, but I don't like missing
it. I don't like being robbed of anything down here.
To the folks who were around at that time, I
mentioned at one point that God ministered to me,
wonderfully, and that the grief left me. What I
didn't tell is that the way He ministered to me was

by letting me go see my Dad. I didn't know if I would ever tell that, but years later, during the teaching of these messages, the Lord prompted me, "Tell it."

My Visit in Heaven

It was so precious to me, I didn't tell it, and I didn't really want to—but I am now. And I didn't realize until two o'clock in the morning (on the day I shared it in the service) that it was exactly—to the day—seven years prior that this experience happened.

It was the tenth of June, 2005—three weeks after my Dad went home—in the morning. Just as I was waking up, I left here. You might ask, "Did your body go?" I don't know. I wouldn't say that, but I know I left here, and I went somewhere. The next thing I knew, I wasn't here any longer. I went to another place.

Some of the words I'm using are not adequate, but I was in this huge place—it reminded me of a mall, like a shopping mall (but I don't think there was any shopping going on), and it had no top; it was all open air. The reason it reminded me of that is because it was like being in a mall, where there's activity. There was something going on in one spot, and there was something else going on in another spot, and something different yet going on in this other spot. That's how it was, and there were people all over the place, doing things. There was activity there, lots of it.

I almost didn't want to tell this part, but the Lord prompted me to tell it. I had some kind of a cycle, or something "cycle-like." It was bigger than a big bicycle, like a big Schwinn or something, but it was smaller than a big Harley Davidson motorcycle. It was sleek. I've never seen anything like it, ever. It looked like it was made out of liquid chrome—very, very sleek.

I rode that down this big boulevard, and there were these pockets of activity, "mall-like," on both sides and beyond. And somehow I knew my Dad was there. I just knew it. So I turned this way, and then another, and kept going until I saw him.

Words cannot describe seeing a loved one whose body you just buried a few weeks ago. I yelled, "Daddy!" And we ran and embraced. The comfort was tangible, like a liquid you can feel. I mean, the moment I grabbed him and hugged him, there was no grief in me anymore. None. It left me. After the experience was over, I got up and went into the kitchen and sat down. I searched for some grief, but I couldn't find it anymore. There was nothing. None. Because the joy I had experienced had displaced it out of me.

When I turned him loose, I backed up and looked at him. I had never seen him like this. His hair was jet black—shiny and jet black. Of course, for the past many decades, a lot of his hair was gone, and what was left was very white and gray. But now his hair was jet black, and you talk about looking like a million bucks, that's not a high enough figure. He looked like maybe he was in his twenties. He looked amazing. I had never seen him down here when he looked like that.

We were in this thruway, this big, wide area—like a road—that went down the middle of this huge mall-like area, and at that point, he and I were walking together, still embracing. We stayed that way the whole time, as we walked down through there. And I said, "Daddy, it's so wonderful to see you!" He said, "It's so wonderful to see you!" I can't describe it fully.

I wanted to tell him about all the things that had happened in the ministry and the work of God, and he wanted to know. I realized later that we didn't talk about one natural thing—nothing about a house or a car—not one thing. All we were interested in was what had happened in the ministry and the work of God. And here's something that I didn't understand; it had to do with time. I was telling him about things *that haven't happened yet*, as of this day.

It was like I was visiting him, not from where I was that day, but from the future. Don't ask me to explain it. I'm still pondering it. It was an interesting sensation. It was like you were in more than one place, time-wise. It was as if we were touching the past, the present, and the future at the same time. We were just ecstatic. Do you have loved ones up there? They're there. They're in amazing condition. You should not be concerned about them.

We kept going down through this thruway, and there were people doing things. We went by these two guys I didn't recognize, and one of them said, "Brother Keith!" I stopped and said, "Huh?" Another guy said, "It's Brother Keith." I said, "Hey." They said, "Hey, great to see you man." So my Dad and I turned aside and spoke to them. They were so nice and so respectful. One of them just started quoting things I had preached. He looked at the other guy with a kind of twinkle in his eye, and he said, "If it's not quite, it's not right." The other quoted back to him, "What's the answer to 1,001 questions?" And they both laughed. These are some things I had preached before, phrases the Lord had given me.

And the other guy said, "Man, that helped me so much when I was on the earth." And he started naming things. He said, "Man, that encouraged me, that helped me, that helped me get through this, that helped me deal with that…"

Do you believe that what we do down here affects things, and we'll be remembered? Don't you think you will remember things that helped you? Do you think you'll forget it? No, you're going to remember it and the people God used to help you.

I was so happy they knew me and they remembered that. It blessed me so much. So Dad and I—all hugged up—kept going down through that thruway, and we were talking as fast as we could about this that had happened and that thing that had happened and the other thing that happened—things in the work of God and the Kingdom of God.

Finally, I began to realize that we were getting to a place where I couldn't go any farther, and boy, I didn't really want to get there… But I looked at him one last time, and just like that, I was gone. The next thing I knew, I was back at my house. But the comfort—it's in me right now. It has never, never left me. It's tangible, and I believe one of the reasons the Lord would have me talk about it is that He would minister that same comfort to you and to anybody else who will read and receive this.

In 2 Corinthians 1:3-4, he said, "Blessed be God, even the Father of our Lord Jesus Christ, the Father of mercies, and the God of all comfort; Who comforts us in all our tribulation…." Now notice this: everything God gives you is not supposed to just end with you. It's ultimately for you to give to somebody else, including comfort. Do you believe there is supernatural comfort?

Remember in 1 Thessalonians 4, he talked about how the Lord is going to come back, with a shout, and the dead in Christ are going to rise, and He's going to bring them with him? (vv. 16-17) Well, they have to be *with* Him, if He's going to bring them with Him. They are there.

Our Father Is There

Why should we be thinking about heaven? Our Father is there. Our Lord is there, our family is there, our friends are there, our house is there, our good stuff is there. Right? Why shouldn't we be thinking about that? The scripture says the dead in Christ are going to rise, we're going to be changed, and we're going to rise to meet Him in the air. He said, "Wherefore comfort one another with these words." (1 Thessalonians 4:18) There is supernatural anointing that comforts in those words. I've experienced it personally. When I hugged my Dad, something went through me, and it's like I couldn't grieve anymore. What would I be grieving about? I'm hugging him, right? And that comfort is tangible now. Second Corinthians 1:4 says that He "comforts us in all our tribulation, that we may be able to comfort them which are in any trouble, by the comfort wherewith we ourselves are comforted of God." Such as you have, that's what you can give and minister.

This word of the Lord to us about *Victory Over Death* has been to deliver us from the fear of death and to empower us and minister to us the comfort of God, so that we do not give place to the sorrow of the world. We do not grieve like those who have no hope.

I have prayed over you that the Lord would minister
a full measure of this comfort to you. I want you to
open up yourself to it and receive it by faith. There
will be times, maybe in the near future or in days to
come, when somebody is hurting, somebody is
sorrowing and grieving, and you'll have this
comfort in you to minister to them. God will give
you words and give you things to say and scriptures
that will cause that comfort to come into them.

Lift up your heart and set your mind on things
above.

Say this out loud:
>**Father God, I believe Your Words.**
>**You are real. Heaven is real.**
>**All the patriarchs, the people of God,**
>**my family members and friends are**
>**there with You. It's real.**
>**And I thank You that we don't have to sorrow**
>**like those who have no hope.**
>**We have a sure hope. It's an anchor to my soul.**
>**I receive the supernatural comfort**
>**of the Holy Spirit.**
>**Come into me, fill me, and displace**
>**all grief and sorrow.**

Peace to you, and peace upon you.

Set your mind there. The Lord will let your spirit
touch these things. You don't have to have a vision
to touch things with your spirit. You can touch the
reality of it by faith, and through that opening in

heaven, real, tangible comfort comes into you.
Hallelujah.

Chapter 8: The Death of the Righteous

Jesus had to take on flesh and blood like us, so He could die. And through His dying, He destroyed the one who had the power of death.

When He did, the devil did not know what hit him. First Corinthians 2 says that had the devil known, he would never have crucified the Lord of Glory. (2:8) Never. He played right into the Father's plan. He thought he was really killing the Son of God. He thought he was really doing it, and he didn't realize what he had gotten into until it was too late. His death was about to blow things apart. Don't you know, the heart of the earth shook when the Father spoke from heaven and said, "You are My beloved Son. This day I have begotten You," and glory to God: Jesus was raised from the dead. We don't fully know what that did to the devil and what he had, but suffice it to say, "He *ain't* what he used to be."

Believers should not be afraid to die. They should be ready to die. I'm going to talk about that in detail in this chapter—about being ready to go. Has anyone ever talked to you about *how* to die? There's a right way to do it, and there's a wrong way to do it. I'm going to talk about how to do it right.

A lot of Christians are afraid to die. They're scared about it, and people say, "It's just normal to be afraid to die." Not for the child of God. Thanks be unto God Who has given us the victory over death. You and I do not have to be afraid. As long as you are afraid to die, you're not ready to live. You're in bondage. There are things you won't do, there are places you won't go, and there are things you won't attempt or try. You're afraid, "I might die, I might die."

We talked about all of the phobias earlier—fear of this, fear of that—and really, they're all rooted in the fear of dying. You are afraid you'll get in a car crash, or that you'll be in a plane crash and die. You're afraid you will eat something wrong and die. No. You shouldn't be reckless, and you shouldn't try to throw your life away, but at the same time, you know you're going to go, soon and very soon, right? The big thing is you need to be ready to go, and you need to know *how* to go.

So I'm going to talk about "Dying 101," how to die right, how to die correctly.

In the last part of Numbers 23:10, it says, "Let me die the death of the righteous, and let my last end be like his." This is dying correctly.

Pray this out loud: **Let me die the death of the righteous. Let my last end be like His.**

Die the death of the righteous. There's a godly way to go, and there's an ungodly way to go.

Hebrews 11 describes the heroes of faith. Verse 13 makes this statement: "These all died in faith." They died in faith. Is dying in fear the same as dying in faith? Absolutely not. So one of the biggest parts about dying right is that you die in faith.

I've heard people ask, "What if I die trying to believe God?" Friend, you don't want to die any other way. Because when you slip out of here, the next thing you're going to see is your Lord and Father. Would it be better to meet Him believing in Him—standing and trusting in Him with courage— or to slip over to the other side screaming, with no faith, paralyzed, and terrified, and an angel has to pat your hand for three days just to get you to hush?

What pleases our God? What pleases our Father? Faith.

Say this out loud: **I'm going to die in faith.**

This is if the Lord tarries His coming until after we die. Now if He comes beforehand, we'll get to skip that, and that's okay. But, if He tarries just a little longer, it will be too long for you and me to hang around here, so we will die in faith.

In John 21:19, Jesus was describing to Peter how He was going to die. "This spake he, signifying by what death he should glorify God." Can you glorify God when you die, as you die, by the way you die? Yes, you can.

161

Paul said this by the Spirit in Philippians 1:20: "According to my earnest expectation and my hope, that in nothing I shall be ashamed, but that with all boldness, as always, so now also Christ shall be magnified in my body, whether it be by life, or by death."

People have looked at death as defeat—that if you died, you were defeated. No, you can die right, and you could actually glorify God in the way you go. We know a big part of what we learned already is dying in faith. Dying in faith means dying with courage and dying in expectation of good, dying with confidence about what's on the other side and Who is on the other side. Why should I fear when I am so confident about what's happening, and where I'm going, and Who is there, and what's going to happen next? What have I to fear? What have I to dread, leaning on the everlasting arms? In verse 21 he said, "For to me to live is Christ, and to die is... *the end? The worst thing that could happen to you? Loss?*" No, it's gain!

Even the church world uses the word "loss" continually in talking about death. But that's talking like unbelievers.

What happens when you die? We've studied this. Ecclesiastes says that the body returns to the dust that it came from, but the spirit returns to God Who created it. (12:7) The Bible tells us that when the spirit leaves the body, the body is dead. It's just like pulling a hand out of a glove, or like pulling your foot out of a boot, when the spirit leaves the body.

People get confused and ask, "If you never get sick, how will you die?" Well, like I said, if you pull your hand out of a glove, do you have to stab the glove or shoot it to make it stop moving? There is no life in that glove apart from your hand. And when your spirit leaves your body, you don't have to put cancer on it or destroy its heart or do something to it. It won't have any life in it. All you have to do is leave your body, and it will be dead. Soon and very soon, you and I are going to leave this body.

We have a job to do, so we shouldn't rush it. Even if you live to be 120 years old, it's going to come and go so quickly. Don't try to rush it; it will be done soon enough. But, when it is time to go, I want you to be ready—to know how to face death, and to know how to die.

We've already talked about dying in faith. Is that different from dying in fear? You do not have to grip the bedpost or the chair and say, "Oh God, oh God, I'm dying, I'm dying." Yes, you and another 156,000 people are dying that day. People act like it's so awful and terrible. It happens all the time. It's happened as long as people have been on the planet. It's happening all day today and all night tonight, and all day tomorrow. And soon and very soon, it's going to be your turn. The question is, "Are you ready? Do you know how to do it?" We're going to do it by faith.

Let me give you some examples of dying like the righteous, of dying by faith.

Abraham

Genesis 25:8 talks about how Abraham went. This is a good example of faith. "Abraham gave up the ghost." *Ghost* is a word for "spirit." Another way of saying it is "yielded the spirit," "the spirit leaves the body." He gave up the ghost, or yielded the spirit. "He died in a good old age, an old man..." When the Bible calls you old twice, you're *old*. "And full of years; and *went into black nothingness*?" No. "And was gathered to his people," to his relatives, his kinfolk that had already died and gone home. He went to be with them and see them.

The New Living Translation says, "He died at a ripe old age, having lived a long and satisfying life. He breathed his last and joined his ancestors in death."

Does that sound like a terrible, awful thing? No, you leave your body.

Now first of all, you lived a long, satisfying life. That is scriptural, isn't it? "With long life," Psalm 91:16 says, "I will satisfy him, and shew him my salvation."

Now, you'll be tempted to leave early, but don't do it. Do what you need to do. Believe God and get over things. Believe God to get your healing. Believe God to get through things that are mentally oppressive and hard. You'll be out of here soon enough. Do not leave early; do not let your life be cut short. The Lord paid for your healing and long life, so it belongs to you.

Run your full race, finish your whole course, and *then and only then*—when you're old (biblically old), satisfied, have "seen it all and done it all," have "been there" and wrote a book about it, and you've done everything that you had in your heart that you were supposed to do, and you've helped everybody that you thought you were supposed to help, and you've accomplished what God put in your heart—*then and only then*, when you and the Lord are good and ready, it will be the time you realize: "I can go. I can leave."

The Bible says, "It is appointed unto men once to die." (Hebrews 9:27) A lot of people have misquoted that verse and said, *It's appointed unto man a time to die.* People have fabricated a whole doctrine saying whenever your number is up, no matter what's going on, you're "out of here." But that is not scriptural. It's not true, and it's not right. It didn't say *a time*, it said *once*, <u>one time</u>.

You might ask, "Well, isn't that unnecessary to say?" No, because the Bible talks about the second death, and Christians will not be affected by that.

They will not endure that—just only one time. And if the trumpet sounds first, we don't have to do endure that either, right?

The Bible talks about things you can do that will add years to your life. You can actually do things that will lengthen your life and lengthen your days. Read Psalms and Proverbs some time. There are numerous verses about it. In the Psalms it says, "Bloody and deceitful men shall not live out half their days." (55:23) There are some ways of living and doing things that will cut your life in half. It isn't God's will; it isn't God's plan, and it doesn't please Him, but it's what you choose to do with it. So no, there's not a "click" on the clock, and your number is up. That's not right.

But there is a season and a time of life when you know you've finished what you need to do. The Bible says in Job 5:26, "Thou shalt come to thy grave in a full age, like as a shock of corn cometh in his season."

There's a time when the corn is not ready: it's not developed, it's still green, and it's not time. But then there's a time when it is fully developed: the husk is dry, and it's the right time to harvest it. And there's a time in your life and in my life when we're still too green, and it's not time. We need to live. There are things we need to do, things we need to complete. But then there will come a time, if the Lord tarries His coming, when you know that you know, "I can go home now! I can go. I can leave here."

Do you have to dread it? Do you have to be afraid of it? No, you don't. You could do like Abraham: yield your spirit and go.

Isaac

The Bible says a similar thing about Isaac. Genesis 35:29 says, "And Isaac gave up the ghost, and died, and was gathered unto his people, being old and full of days." He was gathered to his people.

Do you have relatives in heaven? Parents or grandparents or siblings or friends? Do you want to see them again? Do you dread seeing them again? Why would you dread dying? Because that's what's involved. You'll leave here, and you won't be with us, but you'll be with them.

Not only that—you have family you've never met. You have a great, great, great, great, great, great grandpa who you never knew existed. You're going to meet him, and you're going to say, "Wow! It seems like I should know you..."

He will say, "Yes, I'm your great, great, great, great, great, great grandpa." And you might really, really like him.

Besides that, the whole bunch is family. Moses, Elijah, David. Think about this: You're hanging with David, and he says, "Let me play this for you," and he sings one of his psalms to you. Could you handle that? Are you *dreading* that? Are you *terrified* of that?

You'll get to talk with Paul, Peter, and John the Baptist. And your Brother is there, your *big* Brother: the Master, The Head of the Church. I'm talking about *Him* hugging you, personally. You haven't had a hug until the Alpha and Omega hugs you! Are you dreading that? Are you scared of that? Are you terrified about that? Why would you be? We're believers. We don't sorrow like those who have no hope. We don't live our whole life in bondage, dreading and terrified of dying. We've got victory—victory over death. Thanks be unto God Who has given us the victory over death, through our Lord Jesus Christ.

Jacob

One of my favorite examples is in Genesis 49, where it talks about Jacob's departure. I think it's a perfect example of the death of the righteous, of dying right. I encourage you to read it sometime. Jacob calls his sons and his family because he knows he's about to go. He talks to them for a little while, and he prophesies over them. He prays over them, and he speaks over them. He talks about what's going to happen and what they need to do. He warns them about some things, and he instructs them about some things. And then when he's good and done, verse 33 says, "And when Jacob had made an end of commanding his sons, he gathered up his feet into the bed, and yielded up the ghost," left that place, "and was gathered unto his people." He went on and saw his people that had already gone home before. That is the way to do it!

You don't have to be out of your head with drugs. You don't have to be in anguish, fighting desperately to cling to the next breath because you're so terrified of dying.

You can call everybody in and say, "I wanted to see you before I depart. I tell you, I'm kind of excited. I'm about to leave this place. I have run my race, I have finished my course, and I just know that I'm through. I was talking to the Lord this morning about it, and He let me know I can come home. So I'm going to punch out today from my service here in the earth. But before I go, sit down here. Now, Joey, that thing you and I talked about years ago— you need to get that right and quit messing around with that. And let me tell you what the Lord said about this…" And you just start prophesying. "In the days to come, God is going to do this… and God is going to do that… Susie, watch out about this now. Remember we talked about that. Bobby, you know your daddy loves you, and this is what you need to do now; you quit messing around and get hooked." And after you finish and look around at everybody, you say, "Okay, is everybody happy? Are you all ready? Okay, here I go..." and your breath leaves, and your spirit leaves.

They might as well bury that body because you're done with it for now. The person isn't there. No need grabbing it or clinging to it and saying, "Daddy!" Daddy isn't there. Momma isn't there. The spirit has left the body. And for the believer, to be absent from the body is to be present with the Lord. They're not gone forever. We didn't lose them forever; they just went somewhere else. They were here in the body for a while, and now they're there with the Lord.

Soon and very soon we will join them, and what a party it will be: The Marriage Supper of the Lamb! Can you imagine sitting at the table with all of your family, all the generations of your family in the Lord, all of them? We have no clue what that is. All of them—it could be 100,000 people, your clan. You party, and you celebrate, and you praise God, and then you talk about what the plan of God is now, and what you're going to do now through the rest of eternity.

There is a reverence that people have adopted for death that is wrong. People have associated it with godliness, but it is really the fear of death. You don't need to show respect to death. You need to be unafraid of death.

You mention death, and a lot of people go into traditional funeral-home mode. You whisper, "How are you all doing?"

They whisper, "Oh, we're good."

You whisper, "Are y'all okay?"

They whisper, "Best as could be expected under the circumstances."

You whisper, "I know. What are we whispering about?"

They whisper, "We want to show respect for the dead."

You whisper, "But they're not here..."

They're not even there. So why are we tiptoeing around? It is an ungodly fear of death. We don't need to be reverent about death. We don't need to fear death. We don't need to respect it. Death is an enemy, and it is an enemy that Jesus has already conquered. In just a short amount of time, there won't even be any more death, period. And if our time is finished, and you and I need to leave here, Jesus has already tasted death for us.

Brother Hagin, my father in the faith, used to say this. "If the Lord tarries His coming, you will go through the gates of death, but that doesn't mean you have to go through the *jaws* of death." You can have a passage out of here, but you don't have to go through the jaws; you don't have to go through the torment of it.

Jesus

The greatest Example of how to go is the Master Himself. Look at how Jesus did it, even as He was paying the price for us. In Luke 23:42, the thief at Jesus' side said, "Remember me when thou comest into thy kingdom." And Jesus replied, "Verily I say unto thee, Today shalt though be with me in paradise." (v. 43) Even hanging on the cross, in the worst of circumstances, He could look ahead just a short amount of time and say, "You and I will be there soon." And what else did He say?

Verse 44 continues, "It was about the sixth hour, and there was a darkness over all the earth until the ninth hour. And the sun was darkened, and the veil of the temple was rent in the midst. And when Jesus had cried with a loud voice, he said, Father, into thy hands I commend," other translations say *commit*, "my spirit." Do you know how to die? This is how you die. You die in faith. This is what you say: "Father, into Your hands I commend," or commit, "my spirit: and having said thus, he gave up the ghost." (vv. 44-46) He yielded the spirit. His spirit left His body.

The God's Word Translation says it like this: "Jesus cried out in a loud voice, 'Father, into your hands I entrust my spirit.'" (23:46)

What are we going to do when it comes time to go? We're going to do what we've been doing our whole life, walking with God. We're going to trust

Him, right? He said, "I will never leave you. I will never forsake you. I will be with you always, even unto the end of the world and age and time." (Hebrews 13:5; Matthew 28:20)

Again, you hear people talking morbidly, saying, "That lonely path that no one can go down with you. Everyone at the end of the way is alone." No! I'm not going alone. What about you? No! He is with me now, He'll be with me tonight, He'll be with me tomorrow, and when I slip out of my body, He will be right there. Do you believe it? He will be right there.

"Yea, though I walk through the valley of the shadow of death, I will fear no evil." Why? "Because You are with me." (Psalm 23:4) Are you confident He will be with you when you breathe your last? He will be right there. So how do you do it? You don't dread it; you live with courage. You go all out, and you do everything you're supposed to do. Don't be afraid with every step you take, saying, "I might die, I might die." You *are* going to die. It's just a matter of when and how. So when it comes time, and you know you can go—you feel satisfied and you can tell you're at your last breath—what do you do? How do you do it? You don't grip the bed rail, you do not panic, and you do not draw back. What do you do? You have some faith. You have some courage, and you say, "Lord, You've always been with me, and I know You're going to be with me now. I believe Your Word, that what's on the other side of this is amazing and

173

glorious." And when you can tell your last breath is there, you say, "Father, into Your hands I entrust my spirit." And then... out of your body you go. The next thing you know, you'll probably be above your body looking down at it, and if you have any friends or people in the room with you, you'll see them. And you'll say, "Wow! I didn't know I looked that old. I am glad I am out of that thing." And then you'll say, "Whoa, I feel good! Oh, I haven't felt this good since... ever!" Because you'll be done with death. No more pain, no more curse, no more dying!

Imagine never having a weak day, never having a draggy day. Never again. And you get to leave here, and you get to go and be with the Lord. Is it something to be terrified of? No.

Stephen

A similar thing happened with Stephen. In Acts 7:59, in the Amplified Bible, it says, "And while they were stoning Stephen, he prayed, Lord Jesus, receive *and* accept *and* welcome my spirit." I'm coming, here's my spirit! Father, into Your hands I entrust, I commit my spirit.

"And falling on his knees, he cried out loudly, Lord, fix not this sin upon them [lay it not to their charge]!" I know they're killing me, but forgive them; don't lay this sin against them. "And when he had said this, he fell asleep [in death]." (v. 60, AMPC) His body fell over. Is he there? No, he's gone. It doesn't matter how many rocks hit him now—he's not feeling it. He's out. To be absent from the body is to be present with the Lord. (2 Corinthians 5:8)

Is this the death of the righteous? Is this the way to go, in courage and in faith and trusting God? We trust Him now, and we're not going to stop when it comes time to leave.

My Own Dad

In chapter 7, I shared about my father and his home going, and also about the experience that the Lord allowed me to have concerning it.

When my dad first went home, it bothered me, and for two or three days, I prayed and I sought the Lord. I thought, *Lord, did we miss it? We didn't have to do that. Should we have done something differently?*

The Lord spoke to me. I don't mean I heard an audible voice, but inside me, this is what He said— and I remember it distinctly. He said, "Keith, it's important to your dad that you see this right." Isn't that interesting? Well, he's there with Him; it's almost like He's passing a message to me. "It's important to your dad…" well, I guess He's talking to him, "It's important to your dad that you see this right. You are seeing this as failure and defeat, and it's not." And I thought, *Okay, how do I see this? What, Lord?* He said, "Your dad died in faith facing

175

his fear, in courage." Another way of saying it—as they say down in Texas, "He died with his boots on."

People ask, "What if I die trying to believe God?" You don't want to die any other way, Honeychild. As soon as you get out of here, you're going to see Him, right? You want to be standing and believing God. You want to see Him and say, "Father, I was doing the best I knew how."

He'll say, "I know, I know, come here. Come here and sit down right here with me. You were doing good, baby. Now you and I don't have to think about it anymore." Right?

He died facing it; he died in courage.

Live and Die in Faith and Courage

Dying is not the worst thing that can happen to a child of God. Cowering, living in fear, and living in bondage is no way to live. You live in faith, and you live with courage. You die in faith, and you die with courage. You don't recoil, you don't cringe, and you're not terrified. You say, "Jesus has been here before me. He has faced this down. He has defeated the one that had the power of death. He already tasted death for me. He's with me right now, and He'll be with me all through this thing. I will not fear because You are with me."

Are you ready to go, to die? You might say, "Not
today." I didn't say *today*, or even next week, but
I'm telling you, it will be here soon. If you live
another 75 years, it's going to be here quickly. Are
you ready? It's time to show some of the faith
courage when you talk about this. You're not going
to be a little wimpy, whiny baby or a scaredy-cat:
"Oh God, oh God, I'm going to die, I'm going to
die!" You should have known that all your life. No,
we're going to die like men of God, women of God.
We're going to die like the righteous. We're going
to die in faith, with courage. We're going to die
right—a death that glorifies God.

Even the soldiers that were standing near the cross,
when they saw Jesus die, they glorified God. They
said, "He had to be the Son of God." (Matthew
27:54) Jesus had told Peter His death was going to
glorify God.

Way to Go!

Anybody that's around you when you go can hear
about it or see it, and their first response can be,
"Glory to God! Now *that's* the way to go!" That's
the way to go: you live in faith, and you die in faith.
You live right, and you die right. You go to be with
Jesus.

The Bible says in Romans 14:7-8, "For none of us
liveth to himself, and no man dieth to himself." I'm
not dying *to* myself or *by* myself. "For whether we
live, we live unto the Lord; and whether we die, we

die unto the Lord: whether we live therefore, or die, we are the Lord's." Right? As I live, I'm His, and when I die, I'm His. I live with Him. I die with Him.

First Thessalonians 5:10 talks about this. "Who died for us, that, whether we wake or sleep, we should live together with Him."

I know I've said this repeatedly, but let me say it again: To be present in the body is to be absent from the Lord. And to leave the body and depart the body is to be present with the Lord. Absent from the body, but present with the Lord. (2 Corinthians 5:6,8)

Precious in His Sight

In Psalm 116:15, David describes what death is to the Lord. What does he say it is? Ugly, awful, scary, terrible? What does the Lord say about the time you and I leave here and go to be with Him? "Precious in the sight of the Lord is the death of his saints." Are you His? Are you one of His?

Now this is a thought, isn't it: The Father, Who knows the end from the beginning, knows you're just about to leave the body on earth and come to be with Him in His presence, personally, and it's precious to Him. His child is coming to be with Him now, and it pleases Him. It is precious and valuable to Him. He's been with us, and we've been with Him by faith. We've experienced the presence of the Spirit, but we have not experienced being at His throne.

Think about your relatives—I'm sure they'll know some of what is happening, and amongst your friends and relatives they'll say, "Susie is coming! Susie is coming!" and they'll all be there to meet you. "Joe is coming... Bobby is coming..." The Father thinks about you, and it's precious to Him. He's glad to see you come. Why would that be terrifying? It's not. It's wonderful!

Say this out loud:
Precious in the sight of the Lord is my death. I go to be with Him. Glory to God.

How are you going to die? Do you know how to die? Yes, you do. You die just like you live: in faith, by faith, with courage, with confidence, knowing He will be right there, knowing what's waiting for you on the other side, with no fear, just faith. And at the right time, whether you say it inside yourself or out loud, you will say, "Father, into Your hands I entrust my spirit," and you yield the spirit and get out of here. Glory to God!

This is the way of all the earth. It's not something to fear. Most folks just watch too much TV, and they read and hear way too much junk, and it has affected their mind, so they look at death like the unsaved world looks at death.

No, get these truths in your heart, in your mind, and in your mouth. Talk them the rest of the day, talk them tonight, and talk them tomorrow. Listen to and watch the messages that feed your faith until it just becomes a permanent, engraved part in your heart— so you only think like this. And I'm telling you, you will be a strength to your family through every home going, through every funeral, and through every situation. When people are cracking and falling apart, you'll go in and bring your faith with you, and it will be a stabilizer. It will be a strength to the whole family and to the whole situation.

Years ago when my dad had a massive heart attack—and he was healed and lived years after that—but when it first happened, I flew down and was with him. The doctor pulled me aside. I didn't even know this man; he was a very accomplished individual in his area. He began to try to impress upon me the seriousness of the situation. He didn't know me, and I didn't know him, but I felt like he was trying to put fear in me, and I don't respond well to that. I'm just not going to receive fear, ever.

I didn't get ugly with him at all, but I did not receive the fear. The doctor kept telling me, "This is wrong," and "this is wrong—and if he doesn't do this…" because my dad wasn't real big on doing every procedure they wanted him to do. So the doctor was trying to tell me, "He's *got* to do *this*, and he's *got* to do *this*." And I said, "Well, sir, he may not do all of that…" And boy, he raised his voice and said, "Don't you understand? He will die!" I said, "Well, he's not afraid to die." And he was shocked. He just took a step back and looked at me like he had never heard anything like that before, like he didn't know how to respond to that.

If you're not afraid to die, it changes everything. My dad did a few things the doctor said to do, but a lot of things he didn't do. But God healed him, and he completely recovered and lived for years before he went home later.

Say this out loud:
I'm not afraid to die. I live in faith, not fear.
I'll die in faith. No fear.
Thanks be unto God Who gives me the victory
through my Lord Jesus Christ. Praise God

Works Cited: Bibles

Amplified Bible, Classic Edition. Copyright © 1954, 1958, 1962, 1964, 1965, 1987 by The Lockman Foundation.

Complete Jewish Bible. Copyright © 1998 by David H. Stern. All Rights Reserved.

Easy to Read Version. © 2001 by World Bible Translation Center. All Rights Reserved.

God's Word Translation is a copyrighted work of God's Word to the Nations. Quotations are used by permission.

Good News Translation, Copyright © 1992 by American Bible Society.

Holy Bible, New International Version®. NIV®. Copyright © 1973, 1978, 1984 by International Bible Society. Used by permission of Zondervan. All rights reserved.

Holy Bible, New Living Translation, Copyright © 1996. Used by permission of Tyndale House Publishers, Inc., Wheaton, IL 60189 USA. All rights reserved.

King James Version, public domain. All Scripture quotations, unless otherwise indicated, are taken from the King James Version of the Bible.